Iraqi Americans

The Lives of the Artists

Weam Namou

HERMiZ
PUBLiSHING

Library of Congress Cataloging-in-Publication Data:
2 0 1 5 9 1 5 6 1 8

Namou, Weam
Iraqi Americans: The Lives of the Artists (nonfiction)

ISBN 978-0-9776790-1-0 (paperback)

First Edition

Iraqi Americans Series: Book Three

Published in the United States of America by:
Hermiz Publishing, Inc.
Sterling Heights, MI

With the support of the Iraqi Artists Association
a nonprofit organization
www.IraqiArtists.org

Contents

ACKNOWLEDGEMENTS

To Iraqi artists. Many have had to abandon their birth country and live in diaspora. The rest remain in Iraq and suffer persecution, an unstable country, and a hopeless future.

INTRODUCTION

The Arab and Chaldean Council invited me in autumn of 2008 to be part of a panel to discuss the effects of war on Iraqi women's lives. Our discussion would precede a play called *9 Parts of Desire*, which at first I assumed was based on the book, *Nine Parts of Desire: The Hidden World of Islamic Women*, but it turned out to be a play written by Iraqi American playwright and actress Heather Raffo.

Nine Parts of Desire is about the lives of nine Iraqi women and their struggles in times of war. The first character in the play is Mulaya, a professional mourner who delivers a eulogy and leads the lamentation of women at funerals. The second character is Layal.

"This character is based on Layla Al Attar, a famous and much beloved painter," Doctor Evone Barkho whispered to me. "She died in 1993, along with her husband, after her house was bombed by a US missile."

That name and story sounded familiar. A brief moment later, I remembered that my husband had told me about Layla Al Attar's greatness as an artist and leader. His first cousin's wife was childhood friends with Layla's two daughters. As neighbors, the girls went to the same schools and maintained contact through adulthood, even after they moved to the United States.

I watched the play with intrigue, but I could not recognize the Layla that my husband described. The Layla portrayed in this play drank too much, prostituted herself, and behaved somewhat insane. In fact, all of the nine women characters had clichéd abusive and pitiable personalities.

After the play ended, the speakers, which included myself and Doctor Barkho, took our seats in front of the stage. The moderator introduced to the audience the four women on the panel and explained that each one would share her personal story as an Iraqi American woman. I began first.

"In the mid-1990s, I was on transit at Heathrow Airport when I entered a bookstore and saw a rack of novels about Middle Eastern women written by Western authors," I said. "Each front cover showed a veiled woman in distress and on the back, a synopsis told of her attempts to flee from an abusive husband, father, or brother. I was disturbed that that was the only type of lifestyle displayed for the public since I didn't personally know a woman, not in America or the Middle East, who lived under such circumstances, although I realized they did exist everywhere.

"When I returned to America, I searched for books, articles, and movies that depicted stories with either influential or simply everyday Middle Easterners, stories that portrayed the healthier or more realistic part of the Arab world. To my surprise, there were hardly any out there. From that point on, I was determined to write nothing but true life stories and reports about the people and culture of that region, specifically Iraq, because I know the dangers of stereotyping."

After a short pause, I continued.

"Iraqi women have been victimized outside of war. The war on women in Iraq started long before the bombs fell in her country. It started with these stereotypical images that try to take away her power. Throughout much of recent history, Iraq was one of the most progressive countries in the Middle East for women, with Iraqi women and girls enjoying more freedoms and rights than the women of neighboring countries. Most people are not aware of the fact that writing was invented in that ancient land. Two important women whom few have heard of are from that region: Enheduanna, the first recorded writer in history, and Kubaba, the first recorded woman ruler.

"Stereotyping has played a crucial role in these women's lives, making it difficult for Westerners to imagine that Iraqi women have anything to offer since they're in a constant need to be rescued. That mentality has contributed to her oppression. Rather than get the opportunity to express herself, share her talents, or even pass on her wisdom, she is forced to constantly defend herself."

The next speaker was Doctor Evone Barkho. She had treated women and children wounded and affected by the Gulf War and the sanctions.

I returned home that night and did research on Layla Al Attar. I learned that she was born in 1944 in Baghdad. An Iraqi artist and painter, she was the director of the Iraqi National Art Museum, she had accomplished five one-woman shows in Iraq, and she took part in all national and other collective exhibitions in the country and abroad.

On June 27, 1993, Layla, along with her husband and housekeeper, died because of a bombing raid led by the United States missile attack on Baghdad, which was ordered by President Bill Clinton in retaliation for an assassination attempt on George H. W. Bush. The March 23, 2008 issue of *Newsweek* ran an article where the Pentagon admitted the plot to kill Bush was a hoax.

American media reported that the missiles were intended to demolish the headquarters of the *Mukhabarat*, the Iraqi intelligence services, in central Baghdad. Twenty missiles hit the agency complex while three missed their targets and fell on residential houses in Harithiya and Mansour areas, killing eight civilians unrelated to the Intelligence headquarters. One of the houses belonged to Layla. The missile landed inside her bedroom.

Iraqi news channels announced that Layla was killed by a precision-guided missile since she was responsible for creating the mosaic of George Bush Sr.'s face on the steps of Al Rashid Hotel, over which Iraqis and people from all over the world walked on upon entering. Some people say this is not true, that the portrayal of George Bush, made of ceramic, was the work of another artist. Layla's art neither included ceramics nor portrayals. Others say that Layla did not create that mosaic, but as a manager at the Arts Institute, commissioned an artist to do it.

Some Iraqis believe that the missile was actually intended for the *Mukhabarat*. Others say that a missile intended for the *Mukhabarat* could not possibly miss it. The *Mukhabarat* was broken up into a number of bureaus and resembled the size of a small town. It would be like aiming a missile at Vatican City and having it end up in someone's bedroom in another district.

After my husband came home from work and sat to eat dinner, I told him about the play I had watched. I told him the history of how the play came to be, that the playwright, whose father was Iraqi born and whose mother was American, had visited Iraq in 1993. When she visited the Saddam Art Center, she saw a painting by Layla Al Attar titled *Savagery* depicting a naked woman holding onto a tree. The painter gave her the inspiration to make this play.

I told him that Layla was the prominent character of the play, and that while he had mentioned her talents and greatness, he had not told me the rest—that she was promiscuous and that her husband had caught her with another man so he pulled a gun out and shot her.

My husband listened with an expression that was at first confused, then intense. He finally said, "That never happened."

"It didn't?"

"No."

"But the author is reported to have spent ten years interviewing Iraqi women and used that information to write the play."

"Layla was a very beautiful, elegant, and kind woman," he said, matter-of-factly. "Everyone knew that. She was none of the things you just described."

This intensified my curiosity about Layla Al Attar. I decided to do further research on her life. Soon I discovered that her daughter, Rema, had moved to the United States after the bombing and underwent eight extensive facial surgeries in Los Angeles and Canada. Rescue workers had reached her and her two siblings in time to save them, but couldn't dig through the rubble of the destroyed home in time to save their parents. All three of Layla's children ended up coming to and living in the United States.

I got Rema's contact information and spoke to her over the phone on January 9, 2009. She was quite open with me, partly because she is close friends with my husband's cousin-in-law and partly because she sensed that I did not want to exploit her mother's name, but truly cared to hear her story.

What surprised me was that she did not speak of anger or revenge about the attack that took her parents' lives. Rema was very hurt by the false manner in which her mother was depicted in *9 Parts of Desire*.

"The writer of the play destroyed my mother's reputation, which is all my mother had left," Rema said. "She even tells how my father shot my mother when he caught her with another man, which never happened! We wanted to sue for defamation but couldn't because my mother is dead."

I knew that she was not exaggerating her and her sibling's pain because, in the Arab world, a woman's honor is a serious matter. Therefore, people seldom bring up women's sexual orientation much less give inaccurate accounts of it.

Rema told me that when she heard about the nature of *9 Parts of Desire,* she contacted Heather Raffo and asked why she had given such a false image of her mother, why she hadn't tried to talk to her or other family members in order to get accurate information, particularly since there was a mutual friend willing to connect the two women. According to Rema, Raffo apologized, but said that she could not change the nature of the play. She did promise to mention in all future brochures and other material that the play is not based on Layla Al Attar's life.

After my conversation with Rema, I searched online to see what types of corrections were made so that viewers would not mistake the character in *9 Parts of Desire* with Layla Al Attar. I only found this statement in a random thread of comments that was not even on the author's website:

January 11th, 2008, 10:02: *I am Heather Raffo, the author of this play. Just to say it is not "based on" Layla Al Attar. This play is fictional not biographical. I did interviews with many Iraqi women and men, not with Layla Al Attar. I was only inspired by her paintings.*

Yet this brief statement is hard to come across in the numerous reviews from top publications for *9 Parts of Desire*, who asserted that the play is based on Layla Al Attar's life, causing audiences who saw the play to write the following comments:

•Layla has traded soul and body for safety and the opportunity to continue painting, and her psychic disintegration occurs long before the American raid that ends her life.

•As a woman watching the play, I felt extremely sorry for the women of Iraq… the painter really painted an actual picture in your mind of what Iraqi women go through.

•I thought the artist's story was both incredible and horrible at the same time… She was forced to prostitute herself out to stay alive.

Outside the Arab world, Layla Al Attar was just beginning to be noticed before her death. European art galleries were starting to highlight her work. However, in the US, she was little known, although many of my Iraqi-born friends, artists, and writers remember her with respect and fondness and speak very highly of her. Kris Kristofferson dedicated and wrote a song about Layla named "The Circle."

Through her art, family, and story, Layla Al Attar carried her great energy to the United States. That is why I included her in this book, *The Lives of the Artists*. I wanted to honor her achievements and to tell a story that people who knew her could recognize. I also wanted to honor other artists of

Mesopotamian ancestry who are still alive by giving them the opportunity to share their incredible stories themselves rather than risk having others do it for them.

1

AYAD ALKADHI

Ayad Alkadhi's artwork focuses on the culture and politics that concern Iraq and the Middle East. Alkadhi's work is mainly biographical and sometimes incorporates his painted image. His use of Arabic newspaper on mixed-media canvases, as well as his use of calligraphy, connects elements of traditional medium to contemporary art. The combination produces images that ultimately express the artist's perceived existence at the crux of East and West polarities.

Born and raised in Baghdad, Alkadhi left Iraq for a better future after the first Gulf war. He received his MFA from the New York University's Interactive Telecommunications Program at Tisch School of the Arts, and he has exhibited in the Middle East, New Zealand, Europe, and the US. Alkadhi currently lives and works in New York City.

WN: When did your love for art begin?

ALKADHI: I was sketching and drawing as early as I can remember. One of my earliest memories was at the age of three or four. I drew an airplane on the back of the living room door in my family's house in Baghdad. My grandmother saved me from being punished. I redrew the same airplane many years later in one of my pieces.

Art became a career when I realized that I am at my best when I paint.

WN: What type of artwork do you do?

ALKADHI: I am a painter. My work is mainly mixed media on substrate. That said, I have worked with digital media and sculpting in the past.

WN: Who were your influences and what inspires you?

ALKADHI: Arabic calligraphy and Islamic art and design inspire and fascinate me. Also, I admire a number of Western art movements and periods.

I cannot name a single artist who had a lasting impact. I seem to go through periods of obsessing over the works of certain artists. I immerse myself in researching their work then I move on.

WN: Did you receive formal education or were you self-

taught?

ALKADHI: My bachelor's degree is in engineering. My master's degree is art related. My master's degree taught me to cultivate and understand concepts and theories relating to creative expression. When it comes to technique, I am completely self-taught.

WN: When and why did you leave Iraq?

ALKADHI: I left Iraq shortly after the first Gulf War. There were a number of reasons that precipitated the move. We forecasted that the political situation of our country would continue to regress. Therefore we opted to leave for a safer and better future.

WN: How has moving from Iraq to the United States influenced your artwork?

ALKADHI: After moving to the US, my work became more politically and socially themed. The themes focused on the Iraqi and Middle Eastern situation. In other words, moving away from Iraq brought me closer to it. Stepping away from the subject allows an artist to look at it from different angles. Also, absence makes the heart grow fonder.

WN: What has been your biggest challenge in your art career?

ALKADHI: Like any industry, the art world has bureaucratic and cooperative aspects. I find that challenging to navigate sometimes, but I accept it is an essential part of the art world.

WN: What is the I am Baghdad series about?

ALKADHI: This installment references the topic of the Shia vs. Sunna sectarian conflict that boiled to a crescendo after the 2003 invasion of Iraq. The illegible calligraphic pattern on the faces is a mixture of three or more names. The names were randomly selected from the following list: Mohammed, Abu Baker, Othman, Omar, Ali, Hassan, and Houssein: all historical characters in the fundamental foundation of Islam who are also referenced in the division of Islam's two main sects.

The calligraphy is meant to express my emotions and not to convey a readable, or a literal, message. I use calligraphy as a bridge to Middle Eastern heritage and culture. The presence of the painted words and letters gives the impression of a story being told, which is something I like.

With calligraphy in these works, I implore the roles of symmetry, repetition, and rhythm, which is fundamental to Islamic design and pattern-making. When I use newspaper in my art work, it's a backdrop of visual white noise. It's almost like creating an environment to house the story. Also, the newspaper layer lends the feeling of fragility, which I like, and makes the work less "highbrow," which is also something I like.

WN: You have been creating prolific art series since 2006. Al Ghareeb addresses the Abu-Ghraib prison abuse. The Rape of Venus is about the rape, abduction, and murder of Christian and Yazidi woman and girls by the Islamic State. Miriam is a commentary on contemporary Western influences in Middle Eastern culture. Tell us more about the Iraqi Mona Lisa series, which you created in 2008.

ALKADHI: In this series, I raise the question, would you feel differently about the war in Iraq if you had a friend who was an Iraqi citizen living and experiencing the hardships there? To make this point, I chose the most recognizable face in Western civilization, Mona Lisa. What if those on the other side of the conflict were identifiable faces, your friends or neighbors, and not simply a faceless group of strangers? The idea for this series came while watching a documentary that showed the Duke of Edinburgh visiting the British troops in Basra, Iraq. He asked them if they mixed with the "natives." *Natives!* Why did that word bother me? He seemed to be referring to the brown barbarians, not the citizens or rightful owners of the land he was walking on.

There will never be peace in a world where one group of people consider another as lesser—lesser in race, color, religion, economy, etc.

WN: What about the Held by a Thread series, which was done in 2009?

ALKADHI: Although I'm an immigrant, I always felt wholly assimilated into Western culture. Then my family suffered the loss of a loved one. I mourned in the very private, interior ways associated with my cultural upbringing. I was clearly not as Westernized as I thought.

In truth, immigrants are pulled threads, drawn from motherland fabric and sewn onto the material life of our new homelands. We exist in a state of cultural purgatory, a state of not belonging. Or maybe we're split, belonging a little to both places. We are woven into the whole, yet we stand out. We are bold lines of yarn stitched into the fabric of our adopted culture, in hopes of maybe belonging again one day.

WN: What message are you trying to convey through these works?

ALKADHI: Being a war survivor dominates one's psyche. It is a layer that is not easily shed. The topic and the emotions attached to it take precedent regardless of one's attempts to move on. It becomes the emotional arc by which one compares all other experiences, with the exception of the loss of a loved one.

The goal of these works is to convey human emotions through illustration, calligraphy, pattern, and color. The emotions here are how Iraqis feel about what is happening in their country today. Feelings are personal and not always rational or identifiable to others, especially to outsiders. Therefore, art, in my opinion, is the perfect vehicle to express and translate emotions and feelings.

WN: What are you currently working on?

ALKADHI: I am working on sketches for a new series. I'm also working on a new work from an existing series, *If Words Could Kill.* This series was inspired by the traditional art of the calligram. Here, the written word assumes the shape of a sword and visually demonstrates the power, might, and potential destruction of its use.

As a child, my grandfather, Dr. J. Said, instructed me in the use of words and their implications. He taught me to think before I speak and that words can change relationships, situations, contracts, and friendships. Perhaps the art of diplomacy is the ultimate example of the use of words and the outcome they can have on society.

Adages such as "the pen is mightier than the sword" or "if words could kill" perfectly describe this series. A reference to the words "cutting," "piercing," or even "biting" is commonly used in conversations. In this series, they manifest themselves in the shape of a sword, a blade so sharp, it has changed and formed the course of history.

In the new piece I'm adding to this work, the hands and swords are arranged in a sunburst-like pattern, which will add a decorative layer or meaning to the narrative. In other words, it could be a hit or a miss. I am proceeding with caution.

WN: What do you hope to see in the future for your artwork?

ALKADHI: I would hope for my work to prosper and to be introduced to as large of an audience as possible. Art, in my opinion, is a two-stage experience; the first experience is between the artist and the work. The second experience is between the work and the viewer. That's why exhibiting the work and sharing it with an audience is important to me.

To learn more about Ayad Alkadhi's artwork, visit www.aalkadhi.com.

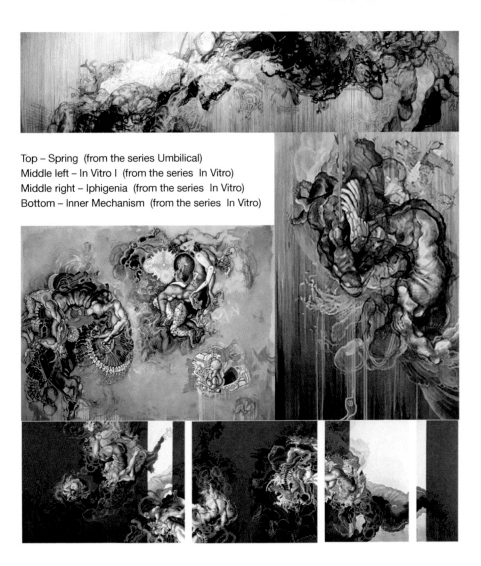

Top – Spring (from the series Umbilical)
Middle left – In Vitro I (from the series In Vitro)
Middle right – Iphigenia (from the series In Vitro)
Bottom – Inner Mechanism (from the series In Vitro)

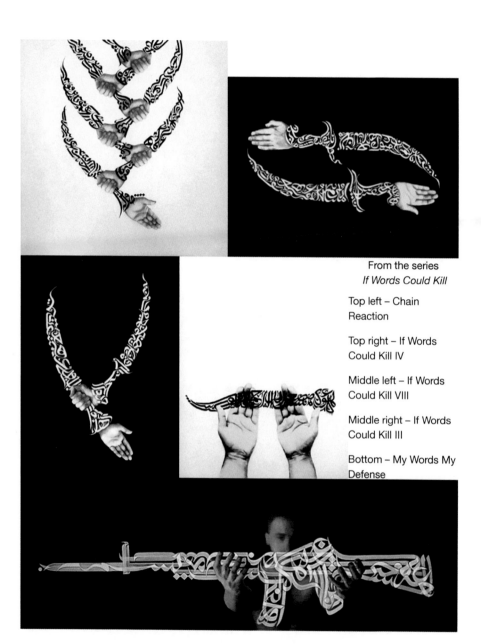

From the series
If Words Could Kill

Top left – Chain Reaction

Top right – If Words Could Kill IV

Middle left – If Words Could Kill VIII

Middle right – If Words Could Kill III

Bottom – My Words My Defense

Top left – Mona III (from the series Mona)
Top right – Mona II (from the series Mona)
Bottom – I Do Not Belong (Diptych)
   (from the series Held By a Thread)

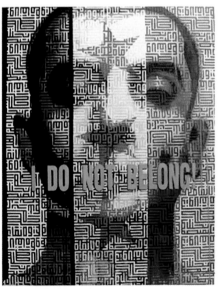

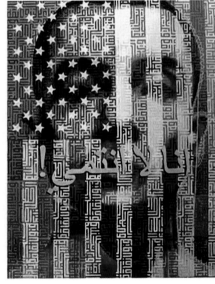

2

MAYSOON AL GBURI

Maysoon Al Gburi wished to attend Baghdad's Fine Institute of Arts, but for a number of personal reasons, she ended up majoring in psychology at Al Mustansiriya University. During her years at the university, she did three private art exhibits. After the 2003 US-led invasion, she began working in media. She held numerous positions as an editor, reporter, and correspondent at various Arab media networks in Iraq, Jordan, Saudi Arabia, and Morocco. She came to the United States in 2013.

WN: Why didn't you go to Baghdad's Fine Institute of Arts? Was it for political reasons?

AL GBURI: No, it was for personal reasons. My father had passed away just then, and other issues arose. I've been painting since the age of four. In elementary, I did art exhibits and won awards, but in Iraq, there isn't a strong interest in artistic abilities, so I went into psychology. I was accepted into the university, but because I was not Baathist, I was not able to find a job. This caused a problem for me. I ended up working at Baghdad's Chamber of Commerce. It had nothing to do with psychology or art, but it was not government owned.

WN: Were you still painting during this time?

AL GBURI: Yes, I did three private art exhibits at the university. I painted quite a bit during the 1990s sanctions, even though there was no art material to buy. I would build a canvas by hand using fabric, and for paint, I used paint made for metal surfaces. At one point, I worked at a paint and portrait shop and made commercial paintings just so I could have access to material and continue to paint. In that shop, they had me paint five commercial paintings and allowed me to paint one for myself.

WN: What type of images did you paint?

AL GBURI: Most of my paintings expressed the violence in Iraq. The Iran war really hurt us, and I felt there was no hope left in Iraq. Iraq was basically a big prison. People would look at my paintings and tell me to lessen the pain and violence reflected in them. After 2003, my outlook on paintings changed completely. The pain and violence in Iraq reached an unfathomable height, so I began to paint images that reflected peace and love to lessen the severity of what I witnessed.

My message is to paint things that are missing in our life, and what's missing is love and peace. This is what we need and want. Take major American movies, for instance, or the popular Syrian soap opera *Bab Al Hara*. That's not reality. American movies are exaggerated. Such lifestyles do not exist, but that's what we love to see. They allow us to dream and hope. They cause us to think about things that we desire that might not exist in our reality. This is what I'm trying to convey.

Our present time needs love and peace and art and education. We are born with this need. It's not supposed to be a stranger to us.

WN: Was there ever a time when you did not paint?

Al GBURI: From 2006 to 2007, I could not paint anything because I saw violence on a daily basis. What could I paint? I could not describe or portray the feelings and thoughts inside of me. It was a very difficult time for me. Afterward, I started painting ugly faces, and people would say, "What's this ugliness? There are no such ugly humans." I said, "This ugliness is of the soul, not the faces. It depicts the ugliness of what's happening."

I was not satisfied with what I painted. I felt this was too little. I had something more to say, to deliver, and this was not it. Yet up until 2010, I painted ugly faces.

After I left Iraq, this changed. I lived in Amman, Jordan, and the atmosphere there was different. You did not wake up in the morning, open your window, and see a corpse of someone you knew, or on the way to the university, see corpses on the street. I felt that it was time I begin to heal myself and the best healing is art, so I started to paint things that have nothing to do with violence, like birds and nature, the sky and ocean. I did this for two to three years and this healed my soul.

WN: How did your artwork change after you came to the United States?

AL GBURI: In America, I tried to be balanced. Many people like myself are looking for this inner healing. They want to feel comfort and joy. One should not always look at violence. Life is good and bad and I must include both, but I don't focus on the bad anymore.

WN: The majority of your paintings focus on women. Why is that?

AL GBURI: I focus more on women because I consider a woman a country, a mother, the basis and foundation of life. Earth is feminine. Life is feminine with all its beauty, compassion, and elegance. A woman is a survivor, always in defense of herself. She must be painted!

WN: What are your hopes for your future?

AL GBURI: I dream to paint more and more. I'd love for art to be my life and work. Although this is already present in my life, I want more of it. As long as I have the desire and the passion, as long as I want my message to be heard, I will continue. There is no limit.

WN: How do you feel about living here in America?

AL GBURI: I feel that in America, there is more opportunity for me as a woman and as an artist. Here, they accept the paintings that Arab countries will not allow. Art is art in America. Over in the Middle East, art is veiled. One day, when a friend saw one of my paintings, he said, "Maysoon, why are you showing her breasts? Why don't you robe her with short sleeves?"

I asked him, "Why not engrave her. Would that be better?"

WN: So your nude paintings are accepted here?

AL GBURI: Yes, but there are a lot of misconceptions. I once met an artist who I wanted to show my art to. He looked at the nude painting and said, "Is it allowed for you to make such paintings?"

"Yes. Why not?" I asked.

"You are an Eastern woman. How are you drawing such a painting?"

"So if I am from the East, I don't have the right to paint this?"

WN: Do you feel there are a lot of stereotypes regarding the Iraqi woman?

AL GBURI: The media here only shows the dark side of our culture. They describe us in a negative way. They give a very foggy picture. After the war, I worked at Handicap International, a French organization. One of the Frenchmen said to me, "When I came to Iraq the first time, I thought I would see camels, tents, and harems. I thought the airport was a big field. The plane would land and camels would pick us up."

WN: Can you tell us about your painting, called Isolation?

AL GBURI: We were waiting our turn in the refugee office in Amman, Jordan. A mother sat there, her head on the table, with one arm over her head in despair. Her six- year-old son stood beside her. I noticed a tattoo on her hand, one of the many that women get for protection against harm. I asked her, "What's your story?"

She told me her story. Her husband and two children were

killed in Iraq, and she was left with her young son. She had gone through so much, yet she just received a rejection for a Visa to come to the United States. She said, "Even this hope is now gone. I'm alone. I have no one. Everyone I know either died or they left the country." As she spoke, the child looked strangely at his mother, wondering why she was crying. He did not understand the film playing in their lives. Her story brought tears to the people sitting in the room. I thought of the pain she carried, of the tattoo, of the many ways a woman surrounds herself with protection from society's harm.

WN: What about the painting called Memory? What inspired you to paint that and what does it represent?

AL GBURI: I read *Shatha's Garden*, a poetry book by artist and historian Amer Hanna Fatuhi, which is about the love between a Christian man and a Muslim woman. I thought of the idea of a woman when she is forced to choose between love and religion or whatever other matters that are inside the forbidden frame of her society.

That woman is Baghdad. Baghdad is a woman who joins everyone together. The different religions are all her children. This is the old Baghdad that had everything, from wars to love, traditions and culture. In this portrait, she's tired, tired of all these issues that turned her into a burdened woman. She arrived to a place of worry, not stability.

I loved her a great deal in this portrait because she represents the old Baghdad, not the new Baghdad.

To learn more about Maysoon Al Gburi's artwork, visit http://fineartamerica.com/profiles/zay-art.html

Top left – Isolation   Top right – The Color of Love   Bottom - Memory

Top left – Dancer
Bottom left – Love

Top right – Blockade
Bottom right – Golden Mask

3

MAYSOUN AL SAKAL

It was Maysoun Al Sakal's dream to go to the Institute of Fine Arts in Iraq, but she was too young to be given that opportunity. She attended Catholic school and shortly after graduating from high school at age sixteen, she got married and left Iraq with her husband to live in Abu Dhabi, the capital city of the United Arab Emirates. She studied fine art at Abu Dhabi's Cultural Center and had exhibits there. Her studies included drawing, ceramics, and wood burning, among other forms of art. She lived in the Emirates until 1995, when she came to the United States with her husband and three children.

WN: What was your experience like in Abu Dhabi?

AL SAKAL: I love the Persian Gulf, the Arabic life, because there is deep love and compassion and friendship there. When I was in Abu Dhabi, it was a desert; nothing like it is now, with its high buildings. Studying there was easier than in Iraq. Sheik Zayed opened a cultural center for everyone, including foreigners, to study there. He encouraged art, culture, and exhibits. His wife, Fatima, was and still is a strong supporter of women's rights. She encouraged women to be educated and utilize their talents.

The sheik and his wife were wise and respected by everyone. They never made us feel that we were in a foreign land. I saw no discrimination in Abu Dhabi. They loved Iraqis. It was the most pleasant time of my life. They taught us all types of art and I benefited greatly from that region.

The Emirates had the right atmosphere of cultural and intellectual people who were really supportive and encouraging of the arts. This type of atmosphere and environment does not exist in the United States. I came here and found a discrimination that did not exist there, especially among our Middle Eastern community. I consider a person a person. Religion is a personal matter, and each person has a right to what they choose. I have no business caring about what a person's religion is. I respect humanity.

WN: Regarding arts and culture, why do you say, "This type of atmosphere does not exist in the United States."?

AL SAKAL: I did not find a cultural and educational exchange with people here, particularly not with the women. Most intellectuals who left Iraq went to Europe. Those who came here were petitioned and did not associate with other Iraqis. The rest came from small towns and villages. There's another factor that limits the presence of a cultural and artistic atmosphere. In the United States, artists need to work in order to survive, so you become enslaved by your responsibilities. Yes, true, there is a lot of freedom, but there is also a lack of freedom. I don't feel free here because being a refugee comes with a big price.

WN: How else did your life change after you came to the United States?

AL SAKAL: My marriage fell apart and my husband and I got divorced. I had to build myself on my own from that point forward. I studied nutrition and natural herbs, a topic which I had picked up from the Emirates. I kept strong. I realized that education and faith are the biggest weapons for a person.

My confidence came from God and Jesus Christ. You could lose your parent or loved one, but no matter who leaves you, God never leaves you. He always raises us higher. He raised me, so who could bring me down to the mud? God says drop your troubles and follow me, so I dropped my troubles. He gave me strength. When He gives me strength, I pass it on to other people.

During those hard times, my paintings were my confession. I spoke to my paintings, but I always stayed standing. A strong person stays standing even when they fall.

WN: Society's views do not influence you?

AL SAKAL: I don't care what people think about me. I

care where I am now and where I am going. The most important thing is inner happiness. People can't give you that. It's within. It's through my faith and inner belief in myself that I was able to have a career and raise three children who lead successful lives.

WN: What do your children do?

AL SAKAL: My son, Robert Akrawi, is a pilot. He is married to an Italian woman and lives in Italy with his young family. He is a professional photographer as well and has two photography books published, one called *The Free Spirited People of Mali* and another called *Unaltered Cameroon.* My daughter, Nora, studied interior design at Wayne State University. She is now working for a plastic surgeon and is getting her master's as a nutritionist. My son, Andy, graduated with a geology degree.

During my divorce, I did not stay in a cage. I stepped out of that because I believe everyone creates their own happiness. I continued to do art and had a number of exhibits. This helped my children choose and follow their own paths.

WN: What is your artwork about?

AL SAKAL: My art mostly focuses on Iraqi heritage. I didn't live in Iraq for long. I can't even go there to live because I have no family there, but I want the new generation of Iraqi Americans to remember the past. As an Iraqi artist, I have to put my fingerprint on those issues in order to allow people to know where I'm from. I was influenced by Jawad Salim and other great artists who painted old Iraqi homes and Iraqi women in traditional fashions.

Every so often, I do still life or other paintings. It doesn't matter. As long as I have a pen and paper, I will draw what's in front of me, even a broken glass. For a while, I did surrealism. Sometimes I take pictures of what I like and I return home and paint its image. Sometimes I'll put two pictures into one painting. Sometimes I'll paint a green tree many colors. I am courageous with color and I love anything that has to do with nature, rain and thunder. I feel safety and security in thunderstorms. I lived by the ocean in the Emirates and the sound and sight of the ocean soothed me. I miss that life.

WN: What type of life is represented in your artwork Genesis?

AL SAKAL: Genesis is a ceramic artwork of a man, woman, and serpent. In America, I found that Middle Eastern women were still not liberated, still living in cages. For instance, at funerals, men are asked to approach the food table first. After they are done, the women then approach the food table. In Abu Dhabi, it's not like that. They have women serve themselves first.

Here, a woman works hard and serves her home and family and yet she is still not appreciated. More and more is expected from her. I reject this and so does God. God loves women more than man loves her. He made her from Adam's rib, not so man can abuse or neglect her, but so he can love and protect her. Instead, Adam simply enjoyed her body. Then, rather than empower her, he allowed her to be tricked by the snake. Eve ended up eating from the tree of good and evil, which was never God's intention. God wanted us to have pure joy and innocence.

Man has misconstrued Genesis in order to have control over women so she will not have a voice. If he were to love and protect her, she would naturally love him and follow him in return.

WN: Genesis supposedly takes place in Mesopotamia, the land which has for thousands of years experienced turmoil. How do you feel about what currently happened to Iraq's culture and heritage?

AL SAKAL: We all participated in dividing Iraq because no one accepts the other. How can we build Iraq if we are divided? We are all involved in this crime. I respect Egyptians because they are united. They brought down a president from his chair. They did not allow a foreigner to come between them.

In order for Iraq to change, to be made new, we have to first change our thoughts. Jesus talked about that. He sacrificed himself for our soul, to renew our soul, but many people don't understand the power behind that. They are stuck in old and limiting thoughts and belief systems.

WN: You work as a nutritionist. Why did you choose this profession?

AL SAKAL: The older you get, the more you ask yourself, what can you provide for people, not just for yourself? I was introduced to alternative medicine in the Emirates and I've been interested in this subject ever since. Nutrition is something very important in our modern-day lives.

Pills killed my father. People are fed the lie that they need medication so the doctor can drive a Mercedes and live a wealthy lifestyle at the expense of the patient's life. A real doctor does not just cure one part of you, but the whole body.

When I studied nutrition, I learned that the right nutrition will improve people's health so they don't need doctors or medicine. When you change your thoughts, you begin to respect your life and your body differently. You become whole. I feel that I'm now serving people by helping them live a healthy life.

Some artists say that great work is produced from trauma and sadness. I don't think that's true. I am most productive and produce the best work when I'm happy and inspired. People who lived before us, those who built the pyramids, lived a much healthier life than we did. They had incredible strength and focus and it came from their lifestyles and their diet.

WN: What advice would you give people pursuing the arts?

AL SAKAL: If people tell you to stop doing something, don't stop. They don't know the talent God gave you and what He wants you to do with it. I never get bored because I'm always creating something out of nothing.

(*Soon after this face-to-face interview, Al Sakal went to Italy to visit her son and his family. I called her with follow up questions, and she was filled with enthusiasm and happiness as she described the atmosphere around her*).

Al SAKAL: In Italy, wherever you walk is all art. The scenery here is so beautiful, especially the houses that nestle on the mountaintop. I said to people, "I don't need to paint. God already painted this art piece." In Trento, there's a cultural show with food and music each week where they celebrate a different country. It's right in the streets. This Sunday, September 6, we're going to the Venice Art Festival.

Here, I feel alive, inspired, and moved. The people are artistic with their clothes, their walk, and the way they eat. There's a nearby café owned by an artist. He gathers items that other people don't want and he transforms it into art. When I go to his café, I see a museum. The owner serves his customers happily. He wants them to feel comfortable and to truly enjoy their cup of macchiato or cappuccino. He does not live for business, but for love and art.

WN: Your voice sounds different from when we sat together a month ago. Today it is much more vibrant.

Al SAKAL: In America, I feel that people steal my energy. My lights turn off. Here, I look forward to sitting with my son on his motorcycle and going out for gelato and driving to that wonderful café. Here, life is art and art is life.

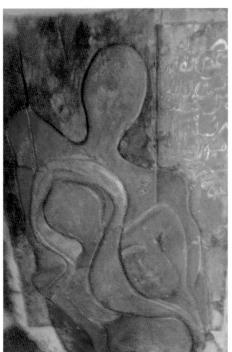

The District of Our Forefathers   Genesis

The Child of the Desert

Old Market

4

QAIS AL SINDY

Qais Al Sindy was born in Baghdad, Iraq, and started painting when he was about fourteen years old. At his teacher's suggestion, he made reproductions of works made by master painters, such as seventeenth century Diego Velasquez, Vermeer, and Raphael. In college, he studied engineering at the University of Baghdad. He excelled in his studies, but he soon discovered that this field was not for him.

After graduation, he applied to the Academy of Fine Arts. He told the administration, "If you force me to be a Baathist, I will study outside this country and you will lose me." They made an exception to his non-Baathist affiliation and enrolled him. In 2002, he attained a diploma in French language from the Cultural French Center in Baghdad and in 2004, he graduated with an MFA from the Academy of Fine Arts. Shortly afterward, he left Iraq.

Al Sindy's artwork, which has been exhibited all over the world, has drawn so much attention that six books have been published about it by various venues including Kuwait Cultural Center and Iraqi Cultural Center in Washington, DC. He currently lives in California.

WN: Earlier today I met with Randa Razoky, an artist who said she was very affected by a painting you made. It was of a man standing behind a woman who sat on the floor, holding a bushel of dates. Can you describe that painting?

Al SINDY: This is a piece I exhibited at my last show in Washington, DC. *Harvest Season* is the title, although I sometimes change the titles according to the message I want to convey. When I paint, I try to get my resources from overseas, my homeland. The two farmers depict a man and his wife. They are standing alone, with no background. A bushel of palm dates sits in the woman's lap. Here, the dates are the symbol of wealth and treasure.

The majority of Iraqis in the contemporary era, including myself, suffered from the embargo and the consequences of war and many, many other things. The dates here represent what we have left to eat, dates. We don't have anything else to eat. Here, you can see the agony and sorrow of the people. The man is a viewer whose features express the question, "Are we going to stay a long time in this situation?"

Since 1958, Iraq has gone through restless suffering. Everyone is causing havoc in Iraq. The good people were captured in the middle of severe sectarian violence. The poor people simply want to survive and live peacefully and all they have is their earth to plant their food.

WN: You received your master's degree in 2004, after the war had started. Was it a difficult and dangerous time for you, especially as a Chaldean?

AL SINDY: My thesis was about Christian paintings from all over Iraq. This led me to take a big tour of Iraq, to visit all the monasteries and different cities from Zakho (in the Kurdisan region) to Al Faw (marshy region in the extreme southeast of Iraq).

It was dangerous to travel, especially since I did not have a sponsor. I paid from my own pockets and drove my own car. Because I speak English very well, I managed well at American checkpoints. I received harassment from the insurgents and extremists, but at that time, it wasn't very severe. I managed, but I did leave the country shortly after graduating.

WN: What messages do you try to convey through your art?

AL SINDY: I try to convey the core of art. Art is not just decorations and using the right colors that will go well with one's carpet or drapery. I'm very good with colors, but art, for me, is very different. I believe that to achieve our goal, as artists, we have to use our tools in art and not simply describe it as a concept or theme. The artist has to be a good thinker as well as have the ability to make art. These two qualities can help you create good art.

Contemporary artists are creating weird and bizarre artwork. They say, well, I'm doing ideas, strange ideas. But I find that these ideas are very shallow. They have to be able to use their artistic elements to create something imaginative to provoke and attract the viewer.

WN: What other type of work do you do to support yourself?

AL SINDY: I only do art. Once, when I met a gallery owner in New York, he asked me, "What do you do for a living?"

I said, "Art."

He said, "Yes, you do art, but what do you do for a living?"

I said, "Art."

"What is your job? How do you make your living?" he persisted.

I said, "I don't do anything else in this world. I just do art. I make my living by doing art."

I live in a very expensive city in San Diego, and I fight not to go to the commercial side of art. If you are able to do the art that you like and find a way to sell it, this means that you believe in yourself.

WN: I've heard that you engage your audience with your artwork. How do you do that?

AL SINDY: In different ways. I'll give you one example. After I left Iraq, I lived in Jordan, where I taught art for the students in the architectural department. One day I heard that one of my dearest friends in Iraq, a talented portrait artist named Mamdooh, suffered injuries as a result of a car explosion that injured and killed many people. He was transferred to the hospital where he struggled against death for one week, then died.

I made a series of four paintings called *Mamdooh*. The first one, I did a portrait of Mamdooh. In the second, I painted the moment he suffered and died, using impressionism style, all the colors in hue. In the third painting, I brought some ashes and charcoal from the ruins of the car that exploded and drew him using those ashes. Here, Mamdooh is gone. He's not here. The fourth painting is a pure blank canvas.

Everyone is well aware that it's prohibited to touch the art in galleries and in museums, but for this artwork, I came up with something new to complete the fourth painting. I asked the viewers to wipe their hands on painting number three. Of course, now their hands are stained with charcoal and ashes. They want to clean their hands, but I ask the crowd to wipe their hands on the blank canvas, on painting number four. The fingerprints on the canvas mean that you're a participant of this crime in Iraq. This was my way of asking my audience to live this moment as a kind of sharing and participating to the message that I want to deliver.

I showed this in more than ten countries, and people insisted on participating in this artwork. So when you see the fourth one, you see more than a thousand people's fingerprints. Everyone wants to show that they are responsible for us not having peace in this world. The frames are cracked and damaged because *Mamdooh* toured many, many countries. I kept it as it is.

WN: Obviously, the war has had a great effect on your artwork. Which war would you say affected you most?

AL SINDY: Each war had a different impression on me

because each one happened during a different age. During the 1980 war with Iran, I was a teenager, in middle school, and I didn't really know what was going on. We often saw black banners in someone's house, banners that said "Our martyrs are more generous than us." The sight of them saddened us.

What made Iraqis suffer more was what happened after the war, when Iraq invaded Kuwait and then the sanctions were placed on Iraq. The very basic, simple food in Iraq went missing, like soda. Pepsi was a luxury. I remember when some Iraqis went to Jordan, they took pictures with soda bottles. To drink soda was like a triumph. The country banned anything related to sugar until the end of the 1990s.

I once had an exhibit that addressed this subject. In the opening of an exhibit, the artist is supposed to dress formally and greet the crowd. When people arrived, however, they did not see me. I had dressed like the juice merchants of Baghdad and walked amongst them serving juice. Some people thought that was part of the reception. I heard them asking, "Where's the artist?"

They continued to wonder until I announced, "I am the artist."

They questioned the reasoning behind my disguise, and I explained, "This is a memoir of a child who endured the sanctions."

I then told them the story of when I was in Bab Al Sharji one day, buying a glass of juice. The cost for the juice was a hundred dinars, which is like three cents. A woman came to buy the juice for her five- or six-year-old son, but after she found out how much it costed, she said, "Oh no, it's expensive." Her child kept crying, "I want to drink juice." He cried so wholeheartedly that he brought tears to my eyes.

She left, and I bought an additional glass of juice and went after her, offering to give it to the child. She said, "No thank you, my son," and kept walking. The child cried harder. I followed them, and the child reached out to the glass, wanting to grab it, but he couldn't. Soon she disappeared into the crowd, but the image remained with me. It still does.

WN: You use profound artistic ways to get your message across. In The Water War, you installed two hundred glassy bottles. All were empty except for one small bottle that was filled with water.

AL SINDY: In every part of the globe, we are polluting and wasting our limited supply of fresh water at an exceptional level. As the population and technology grows so does the demand for water. We see numerous people around the world struggling for the basic right to have access to water, which will be the main reason for the conflicts of the next generations, conflicts which will lead to wars. We used to call petroleum "the black gold." Maybe we have the right now to call water "the blue gold."

In *The Water War* installation, we see many stylish bottles occupy a large area, yet they are empty, devoid of benefit. The bottle that has water is more important than the piles of empty bottles.

WN: You obviously put a lot of thought and effort into your art series. What has been your biggest challenge in this process?

AL SINDY: I do everything myself. There's no one to help me execute these ideas. I even did an eleven minute documentary about the burning of the Iraqi library, called *Letters*

Don't Burn, and again, I had to do that on my own. I have to be careful because here in America, I have a lot of bills to pay. In Iraq and Jordan, I had fewer payments.

Spending months trying to convey a message through art can be quite costly. Once a lawyer friend calculated the amount of time and money I had invested in a certain project and asked, "All this just to convey a message?"

"Yes," I said, but it did make me wonder, who really cares about this message?

WN: It seems that a lot of the Assyrian and Chaldean communities in the United States are unconcerned about arts and culture. Why do you think that is?

AL SINDY: I was once sitting amongst a group of people who were discussing which village was better than the other in Iraq. I said, "Objection. By what standards do you measure which town is best?"

They responded, "By its commerce and money, what else?"

I said, "No, the standards of a society should be measured by its arts and culture."

The main problem in our community is its need to show off. We suffer from an inferiority complex because we can't forget that we came from a village.

WN: What are you currently working on?

AL SINDY: Projects that I'm working on today have more of a humanitarian theme. They don't only encompass Iraq because I want to do something for our globe, not just for Iraq. For example, the last project I did was called *The Bridge*. It showcased the work of forty seven premier and emerging Arab, Persian, and Jewish visual artists around the theme of what "bridges" us to each other.

My goal was to collect stones and bricks and, instead of hitting each other with stones and bricks, to build a bridge out of them that would start a cultural dialogue between different countries. This would help create love. If I love you, I will not fight you. If I love you, then I will put my hands with your hands and we will build something together. All the problems in this universe are the result of us not loving each other. People's desires for opportunism and greed, for looking out for themselves and not each other, are the reasons we don't have universal peace.

To learn more about Qais Al Sindy's artwork, visit www.qaissindy.com.

Top – Mamdooh   Bottom left – Reflection of the Divine Mercy   Bottom right – Harvest Season

Top – Embrace and Confess

Middle – The Revivification of Music

Bottom – Waiting for the Train of Days

Burned Bookcase (from the installation Detritus of Knowledge)

From the installation The Water War

5

PAUL BATOU

Paul Batou was born in 1959 in a tiny village on the border between Iraq and Turkey. When he was two years old, the Kurds destroyed his village in an act they called "ethnic cleansing." This forced his family to migrate to Mosul and eventually to Baghdad, where he lived among Arabs. His family rented a room with six other families. Almost forty people shared one small kitchen, bath, and toilet. He described his home as "more like a prison."

Even though his family spoke a different language, Aramaic, they managed to survive. Batou's mother was forced to work like a slave in a hotel while his father traveled back and forth from Baghdad to the north in order to restore their land. He could not imagine working in a city while others stole his land.

None of Batou's siblings completed their education, but thanks to his aunt's generosity, he was enrolled in a Catholic school. He performed very well, especially in art and science. At first, he drew simple Disney characters, and then graduated to Western wild west-style pictures. At the age of twelve, he wrote his first short story, which was a love story based in the city of Kremat, where he grew up. His journey as an artist continued throughout high school.

In 1989, Batou traveled to Italy to study art, but his father refused to finance his studies. He returned to Baghdad and was accepted in a pharmacy school, so he followed that direction. Luckily, the school had a studio for the arts. One of the protocols in Iraq was that each college must have a music and art department to be used for students' hobbies.

Batou has held a pharmacy manager position since 1995, but he also continues to draw and paint. His artwork has been featured in mainstream media, he has had numerous art exhibitions and won many prizes, and he was able to publish his thoughts and poems in his first book of poems, *My Last Thoughts About Iraq*.

WN: Why didn't you study art in Baghdad?

BATOU: The College of Fine Arts was exclusive to the Baath Party. I didn't even bother to apply because I had no desire to become one of their members. I was fortunate that the

43

director of the studio in the pharmacy school was one of the most famous Iraqi artists, named Abdul Ellah Yassin. That's how I practiced and learned art in a more professional fashion. It was as if I'd missed something and then found it. I was hungry to absorb all the knowledge I could in art.

WN: While living in Iraq, did you have any serious encounters with the Baath Party?

BATOU: My problems with the Baath Party began after I received my bachelor's degree. I was accepted to continue my master's degree in toxicology. However, because of my friendship with Abdul Salman, a Shia Muslim student who was disliked by the Baath Party, my art teacher told me that, like my friend, I would not have a chance. My friend and I took our case to the minister of education and eventually to the minister of health, who refused to help us. When we asked him why his daughter was going to England for the master's degree when her scores were lower than ours, he replied, "She is my daughter and I want the best for her." The minister's final advice was for us to join the army.

One of my classmates from elementary school had become a powerful person in the Iraqi intelligence agency, the *Mukhabart*. I had helped him in his academic study in pharmacy school and we used to play together during childhood. He offered me the opportunity to study nuclear pharmacy in Sweden. In return, I would receive an excellent pay and my family would be provided with a nice home and a comfortable life. It was either the army or studying abroad and joining the *Mukhabarat*. It was like having to choose between heaven and hell. I chose hell.

I served in the army five years during the Iraq-Iran war.

The first few months, I was on the front line, and every night I asked myself if I had made the right or the wrong decision. I played by my principles, and my principle was not to give up my freedom. I later wrote a poetry book, *My Last Thoughts About Iraq*, which is based on the notes and soldiers' quotes I jotted down during the time I served in the war, from 1983 to 1988.

Matters changed when I was placed in the medical unit and began focusing on helping as many people as I could. We were in a city that bordered Iran, where there was shelling and wounded men every day. That's when I forgot my doubts and questions. God gave me peace in my heart, and I ended up staying in order to help the people who needed me. I stopped feeling like I made a bad decision and I felt happy to be a pharmacist. I'm helping more people now.

WN: What was the driving force behind leaving Iraq and coming to America?

BATOU: Freedom. The turning point in my search for freedom was when I started reading and painting the *Epic of Gilgamesh*. That story had a major impact on my thinking as a human and as an artist. Gilgamesh and his long journey and search for life, love, and freedom opened my mind and caused me to look back at my roots as a Mesopotamian. I became more determined to love my land and my people and I came to fully understand that this is my Iraq, not owned by Shiites, Sunnis, or Kurds. The Christians of Iraq are the natives of Iraq. They carry the heritage of Iraq.

Seeing my friends, mostly artists, writers, and poets whose thinking was in opposition to that of Saddam's ideas, taken by Baath Intelligence or put in prison or disappearing from the university affected my thinking. I realized I am not free. If you search for freedom while under the dictator rule, either you think to exit Iraq, or if you can't do that, your alternative is connecting to whatever makes you feel free. To me, the gypsy culture, writing poems, painting, and playing classical guitar provided me with the ideals that I live by and the freedom to express myself among the people who fear God and pray all day.

In 1989 I moved with my family, a wife and a son, to Athens and eventually to the United States. Although it was difficult in the beginning, the image of America being the land of freedom and opportunity lived up to its name. I found American people very helpful. They assisted me as best as they could. One person who played a big role in my success was a friend and pharmacist by the name of Ira Freeman. He offered me a job in his pharmacy even though I had no experience with computers and I didn't know the name of the drugs since they were different than what I had learned in Iraq. He even provided me with financial assistance to get me through.

One thing you learn in America is that you have full freedom. Humans with freedom will be more powerfully productive than humans under oppression. I'm happy in America, but I miss the friends I left behind in Iraq. I've written many times that I can't feel joyful and happy when my friends in Iraq are sad and worried.

WN: Where do you feel is your homeland?

BATOU: One day my father told me Iraq is my homeland. It was called Mesopotamia before, the land of two rivers. My mom said any land that gives you freedom is your land. I ask myself one question. Could I have done all this in Iraq? Would

I get the same support to express myself freely, with no restrictions? The answer is no. Only true freedom will make you a professional pharmacist, artist, writer, and musician. How many people living in Iraq now missed that opportunity? Freedom is what makes a country and its people great. Finally, this is my land. I lost my home in Iraq. I don't want to lose my home here. The way to keep my home is to restore the world to peace.

WN: Why do you think that America is not very familiar with Iraq's art?

BATOU: Everyone agrees there was a big arts movement in Iraq long before Saddam came into power. Many artists had traveled to Europe and accomplished such extraordinary work there that they were very well-known there. While American professional observers who deal with art know about the high standards of art and music in Iraq, the general public does not know. The United States and Iraq did not have good enough relations to create programs where Americans can come to Iraq and witness, for themselves, Iraq's culture or people, or for Iraqis to come to the United States and do art exhibits.

Since there was no cultural interference or exchange with Iraq, Americans didn't know anything about Iraq's history, culture, and heritage. That's the one reason that the US failed with Operation Iraqi Freedom.

Yet our cultures are similar in a way. It's about new invaders who came in with a different culture and changed Iraq to what we see now. This is a repeat of what happened to the Native Americans, when Europeans invaded the Natives' land and changed their beliefs, religions, and way of life.

WN: Have you visited Iraq since you left?

BATOU: I once felt that even if I visited Iraq for one or two weeks, that would mean I would have to give up my freedom for one or two weeks, which I didn't want to do. Then, in 2014, I finally visited the northern part of Iraq for two weeks. It was the first time I was there since I left in 1989. Things were stable and people were generally happy when I visited. I told them, "It can't be sustained. Things will not end happily."

WN: What made you say that?

BATOU: The government offices were unorganized and corrupt. You can't maintain a society with poor politicians and poor thinkers.

Everyone focuses on the Islamic State, but the war in Iraq has been ongoing since 2003. I believe Saddam was only one person and we, the Iraqis, gave him his power. We became his hands and eyes, his army and secret police. We the Iraqis created the dictator. Iraq for the Christians was not a paradise before his rule. We lived among a lack of knowledge and education. Iraq was always a land of fear and discrimination. Maybe the Islamic State did something good. It brought the world's attention to us. Before then, no one knew or cared about the minorities in Iraq.

The Islamic State has a positive presence in the Middle East. They cause people to examine their thoughts and beliefs about killing others, which were happening even before they entered the picture. Saddam also tried to destroy our identity and culture, but not in this way.

WN: Can you tell us about Minor Dreams and Confessions, two of your paintings?

BATOU: I painted *Minor Dream* in the 1990s during the sanctions against Iraq. I used to have family there and you could feel the pain and suffering of the people during that time. I thought about the kids, especially after what Madeline Albright, former secretary of state, said in regards to half a million Iraqi children dying due to the UN-imposed sanctions that made it difficult to access milk and prohibited other basic foods and medicine items. When asked by the TV anchor if the US enforcing these sanctions is worth the lives of that many children, Albright said, "We think the price is worth it."

I also painted *Confessions* in the 1990s, and this relates more so to the Christians of Iraq, when the Arabs conquered Mesopotamia. You know how you confess your sins to the priest and the sins will go away? I confessed so that I can wash away all the sins of Iraq. I shouted and cried, but I am tied up. I cannot reverse the history of Iraq. It's God's Will that it falls. After reading the Bible many times, I found that God insulted Babylon repeatedly for having enslaved the Jewish people. The wars, the sanctions, the invasion— they are punishments from God. They are consequences of the past.

WN: How do you plan to restore the world to peace?

BATOU: The way to make a change is through what I do with art and what you do by writing books. We become a voice for the people who cannot express what is in their minds and hearts. Our job is to explore the world through beautiful art. Our job is not to condemn Islam, Christianity, or any other religion, but to provide people with a vision.

For me, art has a universal message. Part of art's universal message is to deliver beautiful pieces with nice colors, logic, and philosophy for all humans. My colors reflect the tone of the Earth, the language of the universe, the cry and pain of the oppressed people.

As an artist, I go back to that civilization, that beauty, and ask myself, why do I need to restore that Iraq? It's because it represents the great civilization, the beauty, the knowledge about all humans. My love for the US plays an important role in my art. Since 9/11 there has been less freedom in the US, affecting the way people live and think. One of my goals is to restore that freedom.

Usually artists, whether they are American, Iraqi, or from any other country, don't like war. Our concern is mostly for the innocent people who will suffer, whether those people are the citizens of Iraq or our troops and their families in America.

To learn more about Paul Batou's artwork, visit www. paulbatou.com

The following poems, *Minor Dreams* and *Confession*, are written by Paul Batou and published in his book of poetry, *My Last Thoughts about Iraq*.

Minor Dreams

I am a kid,
Born in Iraq.
My dreams were minor,
A cup of milk or water to drink,
A crayon to color,
A pencil to write,
A book to read,
A toy to play with,
A friend to talk to,
A pet to love,
A father to listen to,
A mother to hug,
A bed to sleep,
A home to rest,
A light to see with,
A school to study at,
A song to listen to,
A country to grow in.
I am a kid,
Born in Iraq,
My dreams were sanctioned,
Shame on you all.

Weam Namou

Confession

Do you know that my soul is full of sins?
I stopped in the rain,
To wash,
I cried.
The rain soaked my Body,
And left streaks on my face;
It did not purify my soul.
I went to church,
I came to my knees,
And offered my prayers;
I took communion,
It did not purify my soul.
The statue of the virgin was painted,
With my best colors,
I pleaded, burdened by my sins.
Do you know that my sin is Iraq?
My sins are Babylon and Sumer.
Why did we hold the sons of God captive from Jerusalem?
And carried the curse of Torah and the Gospel!
Why did we follow Islam's banner?
And the great occupation?
Do you know that the rain
Draws my tears like streams?
And makes me cry rivers?
Each drop hits my body
As a cold bullet
That does not hurt or kill me,
But just scars my soul.
I confessed I lied.
I will speak the truth,
To wash this sin away.
But how do I confess about Iraq's sins?
How do I reverse the history of Iraq,
If it is God's will?

Top left – Confession

Top right – Ishtar Passion

Bottom right – Minor Dream

The Genocide

Woman Wearing Abaya   Face From Assyria

Top left – Along the Tigris Top right – Baghdad Old Market Bottom – Marriage Under Sanction

6

ISSA HANNA DABISH

(This interview took place in May 2008. Issa Hanna Dabish passed away in July 2009)

Born in 1919, Issa Hanna Dabish was a founding member of the first officially recognized artist organization Friends of Art Society in Baghdad in 1941. He studied at the Institute of Fine Arts in Baghdad and years later at Syracuse University in New

York. Approximately twenty art works by Dabish were housed in the modern art component of the Baghdad Museum before the museum was looted in 2003. About a dozen of these looted art works were recovered later on and displayed at the Baghdad Museum of Modern Art at Haifa Street.

Despite his age and a physical disability that prevented him from walking, Dabish did not stop making new art works or thinking of creating ones after he moved to Canada. He was no longer capable of working with oil colors and the oil medium, but he continued to execute small art works with pastel, aquarelle, and other materials.

Today, one of Dabish's paintings hangs at the entrance of the Chaldean Diocese in Southfield. It depicts Pope John Paul II bestowing a blessing on the Chaldean Diocese. In the fall of 1993, Father Manuel Boji and Father Tom Simon traveled to Rome with the painting, hoping Pope John Paul II would bless it. The Pope did more than bless it. He held his broken right hand in his left hand as he struggled to sign the painting.

WN: When did your interest for art begin and who or what was your support system?

DABISH: From the age of five or six years old, I did sculpture from mud while living in Telkaif, a village in northern Iraq. At six we moved to Baghdad and I started drawing. When my family gave me four *floos* (pennies) to spend in school, I would hide the money, save it, and then buy a box of watercolors for three *dirhams*. Sometimes my mother would catch me and say, "Oh, he's sketching again!" My parents wanted me to be an engineer or a doctor.

My beginnings were very strong, although I'm mostly a

self-taught artist. During middle school, the principal made a special room for students who were good in art to paint in and exhibit their work at the end of the year. I had more of an ability than those who studied. God gave me a talent.

Art was very good to me. I worked at the Baghdad Museum, cleaning and renovating clay tablets. I had the opportunity to travel to Europe and learn from their famous art museums. I was also sent to Syracuse for a year and a half through a project offered by the US in an effort to help third world countries. There I studied audio visual aids in education. I was then sent to Washington, DC, where there was an advanced office. The man there was impressed with my work in design and print and offered to pay me eight dollars an hour if I stayed with him. At that time, that equated to a hundred dollars an hour today. I said no because I lived well in Iraq and I had the association to deal with. It's not just money that makes one happy but the community that he lives in.

WN: When did you most experience conflict and struggle in your career?

DABISH: The situation in Iraq became terrible during World War II. Employees' wages were too little to support a family. I was working at the museum and had to find a second job, one outside of the government. We had to sell the house's equipment, like radios and such, for a quarter dinar.

That's when I began doing screen painting in order to make a living. I opened a shop, where I drew and did commercial work, such as posters. I also did photography, which I taught myself through reading about it. I was very famous in photography.

Other than that, during the monarchy and the Baath Party,

I felt no pressure to do what I did not want to do. Back then, the government helped artists. They mostly cared about politics, so unless the painter was associated with communism, it let you be.

WN: How do you compare what is happening in Iraq today to what you witnessed during World War II?

DABISH: The current war in Iraq is very different. During World War II, we were with Germany and against England. There was a strong national soul. Now people come in from outside and steal your home. Or they're allowing themselves to be led by their religious views. Before, we would leave our doors open. No one touched anything.

I am sorry that Iraq, the most elegant country in the world in regards to education and the arts, is now led by chaotic and barbaric people who kill and kidnap. We, the Assyrians and the Chaldeans, taught people writing and reading and art, but they destroyed all its beauty.

WN: What brought you to Canada and how has immigration affected your work?

DABISH: I followed my son to Canada in 1993 because life in Iraq became economically and socially intolerable. In Canada, I looked for galleries for my paintings, but they already had enough artists exhibiting. Then I found someone who had a gallery nearby and I began teaching seniors and children. I trained them to paint. After two years, the gallery closed. I began working at home, in an apartment. I am sad that I don't have a studio that I can draw in. It's my dream to have one. I also don't have the opportunity to draw what I like.

I liked the atmosphere of my birth country and the subjects I draw deals with that country. Today, I'll see something from my window and draw it, or I go to the park to draw a few trees or still life. I don't have subjects that deal with where I'm currently living.

America and Canada are separated artistically from Europe and the rest of the world. True, both countries have museums and such, but, individually, neither countries are concerned with or have the background for art. They are not educated in that field.

WN: Have you visited Iraq since you left?

DABISH: I want to, but Baghdad doesn't give hope for someone to visit it.

Top left – Darbuna   Top right – Horse   Bottom - Amadiya

7

SAMAR DAWISHA

Samar Dawisha was born in 1953 in Basra, Iraq, and lived in Baghdad as a child. She loved painting, dancing, and performing the songs, stories and folk tales that her grandmothers told her. When she was nine years old, before coming to the United States, her father took the family to Europe, where she had the opportunity to explore major historical cities like Rome, Venice, Paris, Amsterdam, and London. This experience opened her eyes and heart to the magnificent splendor of Western art. Her family immigrated to the United States in the mid-sixties, settling in Detroit, Michigan.

Dawisha received her bachelor's in theater/film and a post-baccalaureate in art from Wayne State University. She then moved to New York City and began an apprenticeship with a master painter/teacher, Mr. Nicoli Abracheff, who'd studied in Italy as a young man and had lived in Paris during the 1920s. She began painting in acrylics and then oils and soon exhibited in some group shows in New York City and street art fairs.

After her teacher's death, she returned to Detroit and continued taking art classes at Wayne State University. She worked at the Detroit Institute of Arts and was an installation and performance artist at various art galleries in Detroit. Tired of the cold and snow, she packed her bags and travelled across the United States to San Diego, California, where she met her husband, Chessley. After their son, Tam Lin, was born, they moved to Ashland, Oregon.

In Ashland, Dawisha finished her art studies at Southern Oregon State College, where she exhibited in group shows and had a solo art show. She finished the art education program with a master's in art education. After her graduation, she taught art at middle and high schools in Rogue Valley, at South Oregon University youth programs, the Schneider Museum of Art, and the Rogue Gallery in Medford. She has exhibited in group shows and local galleries in Ashland as well as Detroit. Currently, she is an independent art teacher and she is working on a performance art piece that will include new paintings focusing on her childhood in Iraq and her experiences with growing up in the United States.

WN: On your website, this is how you describe your childhood in Iraq: I danced among the Babylonian ruins, slept on the rooftop under a canopy of stars, and listened to the music of the boatmen on the Tigris and Euphrates rivers, singing love songs and fishing under the moonlight.

DAWISHA: Since I can remember, I loved to dance and sing. My mother said that I sang before I talked. I did art too. She enrolled me in a little art school run by this one woman. I would go there and draw and paint.

When we went on picnics to the Babylonian ruins or other ancient sites, I would wander off and look at the architecture and pretend that I was part of that time. It enriched me. I loved nature, and one of my favorite things to do in the summer was sleep on the rooftop and watch the stars and the moon. Back then, there wasn't much street lights at night, so the stars were super bright and they filled the sky. I didn't know about constellations, but I would connect the stars to make faces. I would let my imagination go and basically make stories. The stars were my pallets, my inspiration, and my teachers.

WN: Do you still love watching the stars?

DAWISHA: Yes, my love for the stars always continued. As I got older, I wanted to learn about the Chaldeans. They were the original star gazers, the original astrologers. I was always interested in learning about my lineage.

When we came to the United States, everyone would ask me, what are you? At first, I would say Arabic. Then, in middle and high school, I started studying my ancestors by going to the library and investigating who they are. It was my own personal quest.

WN: How did you feel about leaving Iraq and coming to the United States?

DAWISHA: I was excited because of the American movies we saw in Iraq. I thought coming to the United States would be an exciting adventure. It was also kind of tricky because, after we started going to school, I realized I was different from everyone else.

We lived in Highland Park and the good thing about that was there were people of different ethnicities, like Indians, Hispanics, and Blacks, so I didn't feel alone. I liked seeing the different cultures. Then we moved to Livonia and their schools had students mostly of European descent with a few from Palestine. Once again, I was a minority.

I spent my senior year in Livonia and then went to Western Michigan University in Kalamazoo. I originally planned to study psychology and I needed electives, so a friend said to take theater. Even though I was shy, I was animated, and taking theater class brought something out of me, the wild side. So I became a theater major.

I later moved back to Livonia because my father's health was not good and I wanted to live at home. I went to Wayne State University to get my bachelor's. I started in theater and then I took classes in communication as well. I was interested in filmmaking. I did a few artsy black and white films.

WN: When did your interest in filmmaking start?

DAWISHA: I always loved film. Whenever I saw American films when I was a kid, I was wowed. My dad got the Kodak Super 8 Systematic camera when we were children so that we could videotape our trips instead of taking still shots.

I used to film my brother doing silly things. When my father passed away, my mom found some of them, but I couldn't find the films I'd made of my younger brother.

WN: How did you transition from theater to focusing on art?

DAWISHA: Even though I didn't major in art right away, I was always interested in it, especially when we visited Europe and went to the Louvre and other famous museums. The artwork, statuettes, architecture, and paintings in the European cities blew me away. I was only nine years old, but the experience really influenced me. I'm so grateful that my father decided to take us to these places. He had taken a trip to Europe previously and wanted us to see what he'd seen.

In high school, I sewed all my clothes. My mother was an excellent seamstress and she used to sew clothes for me, but during home education classes in middle school, I told her that I wanted to try doing that. By high school, I started making my own clothes. I really got into it. It was my creative outlet. Back then, fabrics were cheaper and better, and because I had to alter store bought clothes anyway, I figured I'd make my own.

I did not have Twiggy's body. Remember Twiggy? I had breasts and hips and thighs. I didn't look like the ideal girl.

I made various artworks where I'd find a part of a tree branch that had a nice shape and incorporate other things. My sister called this "SamarT Art." My middle name is Theresa, so she coined this phrase. Now I use it.

I always wanted to draw, and I started by trying to draw my favorite singers, like Joni Mitchell. Right before graduating from Wayne State University, there was a charcoal drawing class offered in Detroit, and I started going to it. That was the beginning of my actual lessons, but it wasn't until later, after I moved to New York and met a master artist who became my teacher, that I practiced painting.

WN: Why did you move to New York?

DAWISHA: In college, I took modern dance classes instead of sports. The teacher at Western Michigan had studied with Martha Graham. I had grown up with belly dance and folk dance and I remember once seeing Martha Graham's techniques on PBS and I was blown away by her. I said, I wish I could learn that one day. When I took the class, my love for dance was further ignited.

I had a subscription to a dance magazine and one day, I was flipping through the pages and saw there was a dance workshop in Martha Graham's School of Contemporary Dance in New York. I sent in my deposit and said, "Mom, I'm going to New York." My parents were not happy with me, but I wanted to go. I was determined to go. I wanted to go to New York because I knew there would be more museums and culture there and I could study dance. I felt that I was finally going to live my own life adventure.

I loved the dance class so much that I called my parents and said, "I'm going to stay in New York." They freaked out and said, "You have to come home." I said, "No, I don't. I have a job and place here." I continued attending Graham's dance school, and about a year later, I saw one of the girl's drawings and I asked if I could look at her work. She told me that she studied with this one painter. I asked if I could have his name and number and she gave it to me.

The next day, I had time on my hands, so I walked to his basement studio. The minute I walked in, I knew he was going to be my teacher. His name was Nicoli Abracheff.

WN: What was he like?

DAWISHA: We called him Mr. A. He was welcoming and said that if I wanted, I could come more than once a week without having to pay extra money. I would sometimes refuse his generosity and say, "I can't pay for all of that." He would say, "Don't worry, just get me coffee." He was a chain smoker and loved his coffee.

He was very supportive and helpful. I later found out that he was Bulgarian and I feel he was in his 90s. He never told me his age when I asked, but as a young man, he knew Picasso, Marquet, Salvador Dali, and other famous artists in Paris. He had lived in Brazil with his brother, also an artist, for a long time. He got ill in Brazil and was told that he was going to die. He went to the bar and told the bartender, "Give me whatever your strongest alcohol is."

The bartender asked, "Are you sure?"

"Yeah, I'm going to die anyway, so give it to me."

The bartender gave him his drink and he could barely down it, but he drank it all anyway. Shortly afterward, his health improved. It was the medicine he needed. The doctor didn't know the cure, but the bartender knew.

WN: What did you learn from him?

DAWISHA: Mr. A would tell me to keep my hands sketching wherever I went. He said, "Just sketch." He often said, "If you have a good philosophy on life, you can live your life well." After he spent some time talking with me, he would say, "Now you can go paint." And when I went to paint, I knew exactly what to paint. He knew I would know what to do just by him asking.

He taught me a great deal and I loved listening to his stories. I later became his apprentice. That way I could come and paint in the studio whenever I was not working or dancing. With him, I really started painting.

After I returned to Michigan, I got a call that Mr. Abracheff was dying. He had cancer. I told my mom, "I have to go back." I went back to New York and he could barely recognize me, but he did remember me. His friend asked me if I could stay at his apartment until a nurse came, and I said I would. I slept on the couch, and if he got up and wanted water, I would give him water or help him to the bathroom. Then a nurse came to be with him and I went to stay with a friend.

After he died, I did not want to stay in New York much longer, so I came back to Detroit, worked, and went to Wayne State University, taking more art classes. It was very male-oriented, with mostly male teachers. They did not take me seriously and made some patronizing remarks, so I realized this attitude was not just a Chaldean thing. It's a Western thing too.

WN: You ended up leaving Michigan yet again. What was missing here that you were able to find elsewhere?

DAWISHA: My community in Michigan did not understand me. Whenever I returned home, relatives would ask me if I was still making art, as if it was a phase in my life. Art is part of my life and that's why I wanted to go to New York. I wanted to meet like-minded, like-hearted people who supported my work. I felt somewhat lost in Michigan, but my home, family, and friends were here. I was working at the Detroit Institute of Art, which I loved because I was among art, and that kept me going. But deep inside, I felt like that's not where I was meant to be.

The last winter I spent in Michigan, we had a terrible winter. Snow is beautiful, but then it gets ugly. There's a lot of shoveling to do and I was consistently shoveling snow that winter. I said to myself, "This is my last winter here. At the end of this winter, I'm going to make a lot of money, pack my clothes, and go west." So that's what I did. I ended up going to California, where my aunt lives.

When I got to California, I got a cup of coffee, sat in front of the ocean, and I thought, okay, I'm here. What am I going to do here? Then I called my aunt.

WN: You finally settled in Ashland, Oregon. How did that become your home?

DAWISHA: I met my husband in California. We became good friends, and then we got engaged. One day a friend said, "Do you know that there's a Shakespeare Festival in Oregon?" The next morning, we went to Oregon for the festival. The festival wowed me. We went back to California, got married, and I had a baby boy who is twenty-seven years old now. We had an old bus which my husband turned into our home. My husband's family lived in Indiana and my family lived in Michigan. For over a year, we were on the road visiting family, and every once in a while, we'd return to Ashland.

Ashland was a lovely, sweet, and friendly town which had good organic food and was filled with culture, like music and art. One day, as we tried to decide which city to make our home, we said, "Oh, Ashland. Let's go back to Ashland again."

We ended up staying there. It was perfect for us. I went back to school there and decided to get a teaching degree in art. I later taught at a school for elementary and middle grade students. Then I taught at Ashland High School for ten years and I later taught art and video production at a youth summer program at Southern Oregon University. I still offer that in the summertime because the kids love it and I get a lot of enrollment.

When I teach art, I always remember my teacher, Mr. Abracheff, because he was so encouraging. He loved art. I feel that everyone is an artist inside. When someone is experiencing trauma, art is the best way to deal with it. I took a few art therapy classes and that was amazing. I learned about the history of art therapy.

WN: How has art been therapeutic for you?

DAWISHA: Just from being able to put something down on paper, you realize that you're going through a feeling you didn't know was even there. Things come out and you're able to look at it and see it. Art is a release for me.

Painting is sometimes like free writing. You pick up the brush and you know where you need to go, but then you're surprised by where it takes you. I would have a sketch in mind and I would start painting and the painting would change. I let the painting tell me where it wants to go. I allow it to lead. I used to try to fix it and control it, but the painting would not go the way I wanted it to go. Then I heard a voice inside that said just let it be. Usually, when I allow that, it turns out better than I thought.

WN: Where do you want to take your artwork in the future?

DAWISHA: I want to be open to what comes next. One of the things I've been thinking of more and more is women's issues, a lot of which bother me. Even in our modern culture, women are not arriving at their full potential.

I was lucky because my family exposed me to arts and

culture at a young age. I want to use my art to help women and young girls, so they can have self-esteem and trust themselves and their power to do whatever they want to do, to get past what their families stop them from wanting to do. I tell my students, if you really want to do something, go and do it. I can help you if you need help. I tried to help a lot of girls in high school who were from at-risk families. Some were homeless. I showed them women from the past who came from impoverished families and succeeded.

Mr. Abracheff often said, "If you really want to do things, you don't need fancy brushes and papers. You can bring papers and crayons and create a beautiful painting."

There's so many ways in the United States that one can get help if they want it, more than in other countries. I feel called to address women's issues and help young girls feel confident. I'm hoping, with my art, I can do that.

WN: What inspired you to paint Ancient Lovers?

DAWISHA: *Ancient Lovers* is based on Inanna and one of the ancient carvings where she's facing her consort as he holds her. It's one of my favorites.

WN: What are the themes in your art?

DAWISHA: A lot of my friends say that my paintings have a personal element to them. I get an image in my head and then I start sketching it. Sometimes I get an image from a dream and I sketch it. *The Guardian* is one of those images. I love figurative works. In nature, like in trees, for instance, I would see figures. Sometimes in the paintings, I add the figures and sometimes I don't. My paintings have a lot of color and light and my art comes from the heart. It's like an opening or a glimpse into the heart of my spirit. If I stay true to my heart and spirit, then I'm good. One of my friends said, "Samar, you're in touch with the mystery."

This is true. Every day I'm trying to discover the mystery, the unknown. That's a good quest. That's where I want to be.

WN: You talk about leading clay goddess workshops and facilitating women's circles and ceremonies. Tell us more about your interest in goddesses.

DAWISHA: A lot of my art has to do with goddesses. My interest with them started when I was in college. My literature class teacher was a feminist who introduced the class to a lot of women's literature, some of which were about goddesses. I thought, my gosh, my culture is rich with goddesses. Goddess queens ruled back then.

One night, I felt the spirit of the goddess and the land and I thought, oh, this is what I'm connected to. I realized that God is not male. God is beyond that. Yet in our culture, the men get to do whatever they want and the women can't. By learning about history, I discovered that women can do all these things too.

In Detroit, I was involved with new moon and full moon women's circles. It was a spiritual practice. I found a new moon circle in Oregon. We meet around the new moon of each month at a different person's home. Doing what I do empowers women, helps them know there's a deeper knowing inside of them, a knowing that they have not accessed. The goddess is within us. She speaks through us if we just listen.

To learn more about Samar Dawisha, visit: http://webpages. charter.net/samart/Samart/About_Me.html

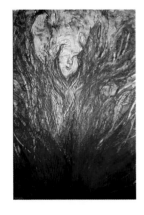

Top left – Fire and Water

Top right – Guardian

Bottom - Dream

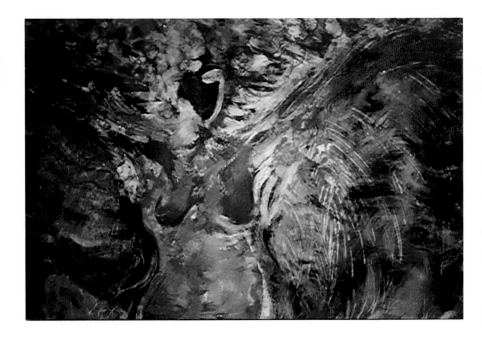

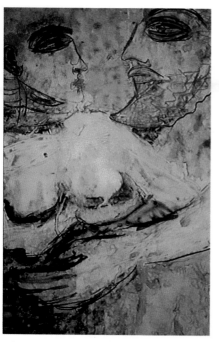

Ancient Lovers   The Old Ones

8

NINOS DE CHAMMO

Ninos De Chammo began his artistic career when he was sixteen years old as an apprentice in Florence, Italy, where he learned sculpting, painting, and designing. A student at the Academies, his work has been featured in several galleries throughout Europe and the United States. Currently, he designs sterling jewelry in New York.

Born in Lebanon, De Chammo grew up in Italy. Now he lives in Jew Jersey. His works are a reflection of the Assyrian legacy and the Renaissance journey in Florence. His figures are produced with an exquisite understanding of the human form. He captures the body's underlying muscles, the skin's smooth texture, and the hair's flying waves.

His Assyrian heritage is evident in his works of art, continuing the tradition in a modern way. His influences are Mesopotamian art, the Italian renaissance, and modern art. He is named after King Ninus, who is believed to be the founder of the ancient capital city of Assyria, Nineveh.

WN: What is the significance of your heritage in your life?

DECHAMMO: I'm a third generation Lebanese. My forefathers went to Lebanon in 1914 during the first Assyrian genocide. My great grandmother lived to be 115 years old, and when I was a child, she told me stories about the genocide during the Ottoman Empire, when they persecuted the Armenians and then the Assyrians because they were Christian.

My people, who lived in the mountains of Turkey in a town that bordered Iraq, had no choice but to leave everything behind, including a lot of land, and go wherever they could. Some went to Lebanon, some to Brazil, and some to America. They scattered everywhere because they were desperate.

When I heard about ISIS, I was shocked. I thought we were over this type of persecution. I guess history repeats itself. Before, there was not the technology to show what is happening to our people. Now you can capture the images on your phone and place it online. Actually, what happened before was even worse than what is happening today, but because of technology, now we can see it through YouTube and similar channels.

WN: When did your love for art begin and was your family supportive of your career choice?

DECHAMMO: I always loved drawing. In kindergarten, the teachers saw that I had talent and would ask me to do sketches for them. I was lucky because my parents believed in what I did, and my father sent me to the best school. In Florence, Italy, I was taught in art schools and artisan's shops. I am also self-taught.

I was chosen by art. It's not what I do. It's who I am. I was born Assyrian. I grew up living among the rich culture and history of Italy. At age sixteen, I started my apprenticeship in Florence. That is where I first learned the skills of sculpting, painting, and designing. For over seven years I mastered my trade in several schools, ateliers, and artisan shops.

At the Accademia di Belle Arti, I gained a profound understanding of the fine arts. I became proficient in creating frescos and monuments at Raymond Riaci Atelier. I discovered one of my greatest passions, sculpting, at Bronzi De Firenze. There I worked as a professional sculptor, creating statues in bronze a cera persa (lost wax casting). I also worked in Bini Alfonso, the famous artisan shop, alongside Japanese artist Harwo Kinoshita. Under Florentine traditions, I created wood sculptures and papier mache masks, as well as interior design and jewelry for Ponte Vecchio.

In Florence, you walk around and get inspired. When I was there, I learned about many different forms of art, and I wondered, what am I going to use all this for? When I came to the United States, I saw that this truly is the land of opportunity. If you have talent, you can make things out of it and find opportunities.

What surprised me was how fast things are here. I discovered that I have to move fast, especially in New York, like run, run, run, to make things happen. I'm okay with this, got used to it. Every day is a challenge and I love that. Sometimes it takes something out of you, but you know, you can always take something out of it and create something. Art without any challenge would not evolve. The biggest challenge is standing out in a world where noise surrounds us.

WN: How would you describe your art?

DECHAMMO: As a fusion of many cultures, from Gilgamesh's immortality to Dante's inferno to Gibran's philosophy. My work bridges historical and cultural differences. I am eternally inspired by the earth's natural elements of fire and water, earth and sky, and life and death. My statues are an interactive message designed to raise the viewer's spirits and expand their imagination. If the dialogue is between the artist and the viewer, it is equally between artist and heritage.

WN: There's a woman playing the oud in a few of your artwork. Who does she represent and what are your feelings about the oud?

DECHAMMO: When I was in Italy, I saw a Renaissance painting by Rosso Fiorentino of an angel playing a lute. This had an impact on me and I combined it with the oud, which is of Middle Eastern heritage (the oldest pictorial record of a lute dates back over five thousand years ago, on a cylinder seal from the Uruk period in northern Mesopotamia).

The women in my artwork are part of my life in some way, but I embellished them. I added more to them so they look more like a dream than an actual reality. They're a combination of imagination and real people.

Whatever I do might belong to me, but I don't necessarily belong to it. I create artwork and it belongs to my mood and my feelings. It's always evolving with new ideas and themes.

WN: What about the recurring lines in your work?

DECHAMMO: I love lines because I studied interior design. And I always loved mosaics. There was a beautiful public garden in my town Zahlé, which had beautiful mosaics. Even though I was only four years old, the mosaics impressed me and I would stop to look and reflect on them. That's what the lines represent. It's a combination of mosaic and musical notes. Mosaic stems from the word music because the Greeks tried to incorporate music in art so it looks like notes and the texture of symphony.

WN: What do you hope your art will do?

DECHAMMO: Although I live in the moment, I hope that whatever I'm doing now has an impact on the future, that it will make a difference. I believe in education and educating the new generation. Whatever is going on around me is reflected in my art. I get inspired by any tragedy, especially when it happens to our people.

I was working on monuments about the genocide to commemorate the genocide against the Assyrians that happened a hundred years ago when ISIS did what they did in Iraq. It was supposed to be history, but it's going on right now.

WN: When was the last time you visited the Middle East?

DECHAMMO: Two years ago I went to Lebanon. My mom's cousins and other Assyrian cousins still live there. I come from a town called Zehlé, which is a Syriac word that means "moving land." It's called that because of the occasional landslides which take place on the deforested hills.

For now it's safe, but it's a very volatile area, and you never know what's going to happen next. The Christian role in the

Middle East is getting weaker and weaker, and Lebanon is our last hope because it's the only place that still has Christians.

WN: Is there a message in your work?

DECHAMMO: My story is like any other Assyrian's story. I was born somewhere, and I ended up somewhere else. My influences and inspirations first started at home, with my family. We spoke Lebanese and Assyrian and I grew up with the Assyrian traditions. Because I grew up Assyrian, you can tell that whatever I do has something Assyrian in it. I'm trying to make whatever happened to Assyria universal so anyone from other cultures can look at it and be inspired. That's my message, and I love this message.

To learn more about Ninos De Chammo's artwork, visit www. ninoschammo.com
To learn more about his jewelry, visit www.ninosdechammo. com/

Top left – Butterfly   Top right – Deep Look   Bottom – The River Dreaming

Traveling Hair

Un-Limited

Athur

Life Machine

9

AMER HANNA FATUHI

Amer Hanna Fatuhi is an artist, historian, author, and activist of Chaldean descent. He studied engineering and earned many academic degrees in art and Mesopotamian history. Through his unique art works, academic studies, and aggressive articles, he stood up to the unfairness and mistreatment of the Iraqi intellectuals, the Iraqi laymen, and the irrational wars and violence that Iraq has endured since the 1980s. He fled Iraq as a result of political persecution. Fatuhi is the president of the Chaldean Educational Center of America, which is based in

Michigan.

WN: *When did your relationship with art begin?*

FATUHI: When they pulled me out of my mother's womb. In third grade, I won an award for my work. The award was oil colors and a book called *The Principles of Painting and Modern Art* by Sadqi Al Ani, an art teacher. The book was published in 1963 and, at that time, it was the only book about art in Baghdad. Through that book, I discovered great painters like Picasso, Klee, Tanguy, and Van Gogh. In school, my teacher asked me if I'd had the chance to read the book, and if so, which artists did I like most. When I gave him the list, he was surprised that I had chosen artists that he himself could not understand the works of when he was a student at the Academy of Fine Arts.

In fifth grade, I started painting Superman and Batman, and by the sixth grade, I made comic magazines, which I sold for five cents. I wanted people to view my work as well as be able to afford a copy of a Batman or Superman magazine.

WN: *Why superhero magazines?*

FATUHI: So I could learn more about the autonomy of the body. American artists were number one when it came to body figures.

WN: *What about in high school?*

FATUHI: They put me in charge of designing and illustrating the school's newspaper bulletin board. During that time, the teacher taught me how to do sculptures. My first sculpture was a leaping soldier with a flag. They placed this piece in front of the administration office.

After high school, I majored in Aeronautic Engineering

at the University of Technology. I also took art classes at the university's art studio, where I received a diploma, what you call an associate degree. I was not accepted in the Academy of Fine Arts Institute because I refused to join the Baath Party. After I received the National Iraqi Award, they accepted me in the Academy.

WN: Who or what influenced your artwork?

FATUHI: Three art movements influenced my work: Surrealism, the French Minimalism Movement of the 1960s, and the Baghdad School that was developed in the twelfth century. I mixed these three styles to form my own. I was also influenced by the hundreds of poetry books I read, the great Iraqi pioneers like Jawad Saleem and Issa Hanna Dabish, and of course, life experiences.

WN: What was your first art exhibit about?

FATUHI: My first art exhibit was in the 1980s and it was named after Charlie Chaplin's movie, *Modern Times*. The Arabic translation of Chaplin's film was *Hard Times*, and I chose to name it *Hard Time*. I used the word *Time* instead of *Times*, referring to the Iraq-Iran War and the outcome of war, which is always death and misery.

The exhibit was also about the abuse of power by dictatorship. It was a political manifesto against the regime through art. I camouflaged my subject matter by using two dimensions instead of three. In one of my paintings, called *The Lightbulb Tale*, the bulb is broken. This means there is no freedom. The light is good. When you break the light, you break the good. If you look at the left hand, it's cut, and there's an arrow pointing at the left hand. At that time, the Communist Party and the Iraqi intellectuals were jailed and executed by the Baath regime. Most were friends of mine, even though I was not a communist. The chess represents the political games. The figure is shouting and protesting against this situation.

WN: How did the Baath Party influence your art?

FATUHI: When the Baath Party was interrogating me, or more accurately, torturing me, as they dragged me to the cell, I could only think of two things: my girlfriend and how to make this into a painting. I ended up with a painting and a poem, both called *Life Wins*. The squares in the painting represent jail, or the dictatorship regime, and the palm tree represents life, Iraq, and hope. It says no box can hold life or hope. Despite terrorism and torture, life and hope can always find a way.

WN: When did your conflict with the Baath Party begin?

FATUHI: I was five or six years old when the Baath Party came into power. From the start, I didn't believe in them. That attitude was largely influenced by my father. He said, "Anytime someone kills an Iraqi citizen, it means they are not Iraqi citizens." When the Baathist executed former president Abd Al Karim Qasim, my father said, "This is a bad thing and bad people came into power."

Although I often stood up to the Baath Party by defending Iraqi intellectuals, promoting the artists that others were afraid to promote, and by encouraging freedom, I was smart enough to work on a thin line that would prevent me from their abusive ways. But as smart as one was, when negative points against him or her pile up, more questions were raised by the Baath Party, which led to further interrogations. They would come and ask me, "Why don't you want to join the Arabic Socialist Baath Party?" and I would reply, "I'm not an Arab."

WN: What consequences did you have to face for not join-

ing the Baath party?

FATUHI: I had fewer rights than Baathists, who would receive scholarships and higher education. For instance, when, in 1986, I won the Iraqi National Flag Competition, the competition was canceled because I am a Chaldean and not an Arab, a Christian and not a Muslim, independent and not a Baathist. For years I was interrogated on numerous occasions, but I was never sentenced to jail. I was, however, sentenced to death three times. In the 1990s I endured the regime's torture for several reasons: I was asked to draw portraits of Saddam but refused; I did not participate in an annual Baath Party Exhibit, which was mandatory. Anyone who didn't was considered an enemy and faced execution; I refused, as head of the visual arts magazine, *Fanoon*, to glorify the regime by writing articles about Saddam and his son, Oudai.

As an artist, I can't have anyone lead me.

WN: What caused you to eventually flee Iraq?

FATUHI: I had lived in Amman, Jordan for two years. During this time, many of the Iraqi artists in Amman—ninety percent who were against the Baath regime—met at my studio. One of them, a Baathist, returned to Iraq and reported that I was an anti-Baathist whose studio is the center of an opposition movement.

I returned to Iraq in order to get my wife and four children (two set of twins) out of the country. That's when, after another torture session by the regime, a lieutenant warned me, "The next time they take you in, Amer, you'll never leave. They'll execute you. Try to leave Iraq." So I took my family and escaped. Afterward, I was sentenced to death in absentia three times. They also withdrew my citizenship. Ironically, someone who is an immigrant, an Arab invader, takes away a native Iraqi's citizenship.

I came to America, which was a dream of mine since age ten. Who hasn't dreamt of coming to America?

WN: What was your initial opinion of America, particularly its art?

FATUHI: Coming to America was shocking because all that I had read, all that I had experienced about America in Iraq, was quite different. Iraqi artists love and respect works of Rauschenberg, Pollock, and Gasper, but today's American art has no soul. It's just merchandise. Well-known artists are made by the media, produced for money purposes. And it's not just in American art, but also modern Western art. Today's artists are copycats of European and famous American artists.

That is why I am surprised that, despite the rich history and background of Iraqi artists, Americans look at Iraqi artists' works as being less worthy. I don't do artwork to place it in my studio. I want to share it with the public, but because I'm an Iraqi-born, Americans don't have enough of an appreciation for it. My work is post-modernism, my major theme were love and violence, peace and war, executed through the pictograph, which was the first writing system created in Mesopotamia in 4100 BC. I used techniques related to me, my heritage, and my system. Americans have an image of Iraq, a stereotype that it consists of mosques, Aladdin, camels, and Islamists, but that's not the Iraq that I know best, it's not part of my culture, it's not me.

America offers me freedom but, at the same time, there are lots of discrimination issues. They will accept me based on their terms. They want to put me in a box, but I cannot bring myself to do that because art and love are similar in that there are no rules.

By Americans allowing various perspectives to interact, they are doing something for themselves. Since they are part of humanity, they have to share their point of view with others. There should not be obstacles when it comes to cultural matters. We're all living in a small street. Although there is law and order, which are very important, there are no borders. What happens thousands of miles away, whether in China, Iraq, or Italy, you learn about it within seconds.

WN: Why do you think Americans should join forces with Iraqi artists and intellectuals?

FATUHI: Since Iraq is the richest country in the world when comparing its wealth to the country's size and population, it's important and beneficial for Americans to support Iraqis. If America supports them, America will have an ally for life.

Art is outside of history, which deals with two factors: time and location. Art has no time. No location. If a Sumerian statue is shown to someone, it will be accepted by an American, Spanish, Chinese, Russian living in 2015. Time and place have no effect. The person will love it and will want it in their home no matter when and where it was made. Art is universal and eternal.

I am sad about what has happened to Iraq since it went under four occupiers— Americans, Iranians, Kurds and Arab Fanatics—but I believe that the current chaos is the result of Saddam's regime. America was just a player seizing an opportunity, but art will have the last word.

WN: You worked in Iraq with the US Army. What was that

experience like?

FATUHI: I went to Iraq in 2008, where I served as senior advisor for the US Army on Ethno Religious Affairs. I had not been there since I left in 1994 and from the start I realized that the Iraq I came to wasn't mine. It was foreign to me. With only some exceptions, old friends who had changed very little who really embraced me, the rest of Iraq was not the Iraq I used to know. People were very illiterate, like cattle of a religious cult. Iraq had a brain drain.

The best part about the experience was working with the army. They have discipline and loyalty and it felt like I was living with my family. It's not what you see on television with the shooting and violence. Those that abuse their power are the exceptions. The military is like any society. You have good and bad in it.

With the army, I feel I'm part of a team and we have a mission. The mission comes first. I wrote a booklet during that time called *Winning Iraq* and passed it out for free to military personnel. It was to help bridge understanding between the military and the Iraqi people.

I explained to the far left not to feel guilty when the terrorists call them crusaders. This is propaganda. This is not the Arab's land. It was stolen from the natives. The whole Middle East was stolen hundreds of years before the Crusade. They were fighting on land that does not belong to either party, not the Middle Eastern Muslims or the Europeans.

WN: What influence did the US Army have on you and your work?

FATUHI: The army influenced me in that I used to be anti-war, though I participated in two wars in Iraq. I was like a hippie in Iraq, without the marijuana. But, by being in the army, I realized that sometimes, for a strong and lasting peace, we have to go to war. It's that simple.

I was in Iraq for three and a half years, but I never quit working in the art venue. I supervised two Iraqi art exhibits at the US Embassy. Also, I finished my book of poems, *Shatha's Garden*, and published it in 2011. The poems are about the love shared between a Christian man and a Muslim woman. One of my friends, Maysoon Al Gburi, a wonderful artist, was inspired by *Shatha's Garden* to make a painting. And I completed *The Untold Story of Native Iraqis* and that was published in 2012.

The Untold Story of Native Iraqis provides a historical perspective about the true identity of Iraq's minorities, specifically Chaldeans. It also analyzes the issue of the Arabs, Turks, and Kurds usurping Chaldean's national identity since the seventh century AD.

WN: What kind of painting do you do today?

FATUHI: I used to do painting on canvas. Now I do frame only. Today you can't display in Iraq the type of artwork that I do. They will kill you.

To learn more about Amer Hanna Fatuhi, visit his website: www.amerfatuhiart.com

Life Wins

A towering Palm Tree
They took her once
To the whorehouse's colors
And to the house of the words' prostitution
She didn't bend
As one tired of the drying color and the ink Silence
They dragged her by her braids
To the basement of torture
From night to dawn
And from the night to dawn
She didn't curl
When they were fed up with the extensive patience
They took her to the battlefield
And from a party quarter
To a detention center
To a lair
She was not beaten, or broken
They said "Let us paint her nails
And braid her plaits"
And covering her with silk, rayon, rubies and precious stones
They talked again and again, when they became so despaired
They cursed the two rivers
Babylon's gardens
And the people of Baghdad who are as nice looking as the
moon
Then terrifyingly they closed up on her
The tomb's door
When I returned

After years of deprivation
Getting lost and oppression
I found on her concrete sepulcher
A rug of dates
And a towering palm tree!

By Amer Fatuhi, from his book of poems *Iraq... Love, Death
and Beyond*

Invaders

Fleeing a Paradise   The First Paradise

Disappointed Ishtar

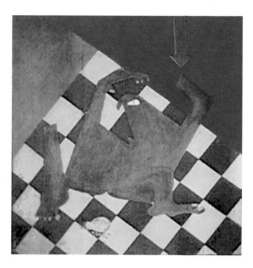

The Lightbulb Tale

Bull and Female

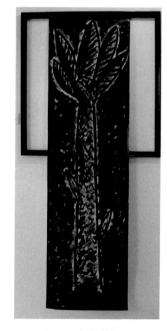

Iraq… Life Wins

10

FAROUK KASPAULES

Farouk Kaspaules is an Iraqi-born Canadian artist who left Iraq in the 1970s. In 1982 he graduated with an MS in economics from Ottawa University. After working as an economist for two years, he realized the need to find a medium to express himself. He decided to study visual arts. He obtained a Bachelor of Fine Arts at the University of Ottawa in 1988 and has participated in exhibitions worldwide over the last twenty years, including locations in the United States, France, Egypt, Jordan, and Brazil.

During that time he has been actively engaged in artist-run centers and organizing and curating exhibits with political and cultural themes. Since 2009, he has been an art instructor at Ottawa School of Art.

WN: What are your fondest memories of Iraq, especially as it relates to your art?

KASPAULES: My fondest memories of Iraq are when I was a child coming home from school and then rushing off to the park to play soccer or other games with my classmates. The smell of the food, the sound of the people, the landscape of the city, and the rich history—I remember all of that. On school field trips, we went to see ancient cities, like Babylon and Nineveh, and monuments that were thousands of years old. These became embedded in me, my personality, and later my artwork.

My interest in art started in secondary school. I would go through foreign magazines looking for images of works by artists. I was inspired by that.

WN: As an artist, did you receive support from family and your community? Who and what were your primary influences?

KASPAULES: I had a lot of encouragement from my friends in Ottawa, who saw the strength of my interest in art. Through art, I have been able to express my political and social thoughts about Iraq and to show my love for that country.

My major influences were Joseph Beuys, Robert Rauschenberg, and Andy Warhol. Of course, I am influenced by art theories, i.e. postmodernism.

WN: What was the leading force behind you leaving Iraq and how has your life, as an artist, been in Canada?

KASPAULES: Like many Iraqis, I left because of internal conditions. I came to Canada because, as with many Iraqis, if a country gives you permanent residency, you stay. You don't choose. So I applied and was granted the stay. Living in Canada, my home now, has opened many possibilities for me. I am able to combine my art practice with teaching. I am involved with my peer artists in art making, exhibiting, discussion, and so on. I believe being in Canada strengthened my interest and ambition in this field.

WN: How have the wars in Iraq affected your life or your art?

KASPAULES: I always make statements about Iraq. War has been a central topic in my art. I believe that it's because of Iraq's political and social issues that I studied art. I wanted to express my concerns about Iraq visually. My visual experiments in mixed media focuses on concepts of displacement and exile and employ a complex vocabulary of images, symbols, and aesthetic forms derived from ancient and contemporary Iraq, as well as from my mixed cultural background [Chaldean and Arab].

My art continues to change both in style and technique. Though Iraq and what has happened there remains the subject matter, my style is more symbolic instead of a direct reaction to the destruction of Iraq. I appropriate images from Iraq and deconstruct these images to create work which deals with Iraq. In terms of technique, I use mixed medium such as silkscreen, photo-silkscreen, Cyanotype, and Van Dyke Brown on paper, canvas, and vellum. I address issues of identity and belonging in terms of violence.

Using my art, I try to engage the viewer so that they can become aware of the situation in Iraq and what those situations mean. Sure, the media covers news about Iraq every day, but an exhibition in a gallery about the situation in Iraq is a different dialogue, has a different impact, because of the closeness between the work and the viewer.

Expressing political themes in art becomes an activity for me that cannot be separated from my life experiences. In my work, I strive to relate daily events to broader geopolitical and social questions, thereby affirming the cultural and the political, on the one hand, and the artistic position in terms of the political and aesthetic context, on the other. Remaining intimately linked to my birth country through my past and my art, I preserve my memories through these images while also acknowledging their painfully ephemeral nature. Geopolitically speaking, Iraq as I remember it no longer exists.

WN: How do you feel about the Islamic State's destruction of Iraq's museums and historical monuments in an attempt to erase its heritage?

KASPAULES: Any group who not only opposes a culture but erases that culture by violent means is committing a war crime. I consider this criminal act of destroying museums not only a crime against Iraq or Iraqi people, but against human values in general. Those who committed these acts must stand before International Court.

A historical Iraq, with its thousand years of civilization, cannot be erased.

WN: Do you think it's possible for art to help establish

peace between the East and the West?

KASPAULES: Any dialogue, any interaction between two entities, will create the condition for understanding each other's position. I don't think there's conflict between the East and the West. There are concerns on both sides that need to be addressed. These concerns are internal and external regarding the East. Through art, and through engaging the audience so they can see concerns on both sides, I believe we can create closeness and familiarity with each other and distance ourselves from the rhetoric. Throughout history, art was always a way to bring people together. Art in any form can do that.

WN: To what do you attribute the West's lack of awareness about Iraq's history and culture?

KASPAULES: Iraq has been in history books since day one. A student from any culture has studied ancient Iraq, but I believe an attempt to altogether erase the identity and culture of this country was made to serve rulers. That was the case with the previous regime, the Baath Party. Meanwhile, the US pretended not to know anything about Iraq's culture, and in its own way, erased many of its rich and significant elements.

The situation in Iraq is very critical. The country and its people are subject to conditions which, economically, socially, and culturally, are very difficult. Before, there were zealous groups on one hand and the US on the other. Now the artists are fighting the dogma of certain groups, and those groups are trying to make them produce certain works of art that do not address the real issues in Iraq.

When I teach at Ottawa School of Art, the students ask questions about Iraq mostly because they know I am from Iraq. This gives me the opportunity to engage with students about making art and addressing political issues. The students see productions of art from Iraq, which raises a number of questions, so there is a dialogue.

WN: Can you describe The Return?

KASPAULES: This work was inspired by the return of the Marsh Arabs to their original habitat. In the past, they were forced to leave this area, called Al Ahwar in Arabic, which is in the southern part of Iraq, where the Tigris and the Euphrates Rivers meet. This region has a whole culture by itself. The people live in still water that is about three feet deep. They take reeds, weave them together, and put them on the water. They place grass over weaved reeds and then build their house.

My interest in this piece is historical and personal. My origin is Chaldean, and Chaldeans trace their roots to the Sumerians who lived in the Marshes over five thousand years ago.

WN: What about The Guardians?

KASPAULES: This work was inspired by Babylon. It's a reaction to the destruction going on in Iraq. In this work, I'm telling the viewer that Iraq has an old and rich history and culture. Any attack on that history and culture is an attack on civilization.

Top – State of Things

Bottom left – The Return

Bottom right – The Guardians

Top left – Forms

Top right – Target

Bottom – After the Attack

11

NADWA QARAGHOLI

Nadwa Qaragholi was born and raised in Baghdad and educated both in her native city and the American College in Beirut. Her earliest influence was her mother, a high school art teacher who instilled in her a deep appreciation for color and beauty in all of its manifestations.

She went on to formally study fine arts in Baghdad under the acclaimed Iraqi artist Miran Al Saadi. After leaving Iraq in 1980, she lived in London and then she moved to California where she studied art at Santa Monica College and also at UCLA in Los Angeles. She finally settled in metropolitan Washington, DC.

An active member of the Alexandria Art League for twenty-five years, she continued to refine her art under the guidance of distinguished sculptor Liberace and notable portrait painter Danny Dawson. In 2008, she founded Living Light International, a nonprofit organization whose missions include helping vulnerable children and orphans in Iraq. As the president of this organization, Qaragholi has devoted much of her life to its humanitarian missions.

WN: Describe your relationship with your mother in regards to you both having a love for art.

QARAGHOLI: My mother was an artist in soul, personality, and appearance, but she was against me becoming an artist. She didn't encourage me at all, concerned that I wouldn't have a future in art, but my generation was different than hers. Some of my friends became very famous.

WN: What was the driving force behind you leaving Iraq?

QARAGHOLI: I didn't leave Iraq for any political or ambitious reasons. My life there was secure. I was to study abroad—to Paris, originally—but we ended up in the US. Once we came here, the war started, so we couldn't go back. It was meant to be. It wasn't planned at all.

WN: How did you feel during the 2003 US-led war, given that Iraq is your birthplace and the US your home?

QARAGHOLI: I felt pain for both sides. America is our haven. At the same time, Iraq is my birth country. Seeing people get killed is very painful. You just sit and feel you can't do anything about it. Your hands are tied. The only thing you can do is paint. Maybe I'm blessed. I can at least express myself with my paintings. Others can't. Plus I had a magnificent community of artists in the city of Alexandria, where I received encouragement and motivation, continuous growth, and learning. When you're surrounded by artists, you grow as an artist. I love being in Alexandria. It's where I belong as an artist. While there was a big movement toward art in Iraq, artists were not exposed to the world. They were enclosed within Iraq and maybe some of the Arabic countries. Now we're very much in demand.

WN: What works have inspired you?

QARAGHOLI: *The Rubaiyat of Omar Al Khayyam.* It was written in the thirteenth century, a time when oppression denied the poet open expression. Omar Al Khayyam's brilliant use of metaphor was the cloak through which he relayed his indignation at suppression and its injustice and cost. I have borrowed his cloak, embedding images behind paint as a voiceless testament to the human spirit's cry against subjugation.

In one of my art series, inspired by Omar Khayyam's *Rubaiyat*, I embarked on a journey of dream exploration, one intimately tied to the present in as much as it calls forth the past. My paintings are a narration of my innermost thoughts. Very much the way a writer uses his pen, I use my brush to confide a story to my canvas, into which I investigate what is intangible and elusive.

This series of work is based upon my life's experience coupled with the poetry of Omar Al Khayyam. It is a gateway to the unconscious level of dreams. Like the archeologist who digs with diligence and delicately dusts precious remnants from another time, I am searching for fragments of the past

to decipher my feelings of the present. I apply my paint soft-
ly, layering transparent veils of color so as not to disturb the
dream.

*WN: You once said that you feel connected to Gibran
Khalil Gibran. How so?*

QARAGHOLI: While a strong believer in God, I am always against labels, which can be harmful. I prefer, instead, to
see the goodness in people and not their labels. In this way, I
feel I resemble Gibran Khalil Gibran, who has been my biggest influence in regards to my thoughts. I've always felt he
was beyond nationality and religion, so I connected to him. I
am similar to him.

WN: How would you describe yourself as an artist?

QARAGHOLI: It takes forever for me to finish a painting
because I put my heart into it, I really do. My goal is not to
finish one. My goal is to say, or change, something. I try to
express women's issues and my dissatisfaction with women's
issues.

Even when I'm not drawing, I'm drawing. I'm one of
those who can see faces in everything: in curtains, in the marble, the grain of the marble. Everywhere.

WN: How did your art change over the years?

QARAGHOLI: My parents were US citizens but lived in
Iraq. They didn't feel they belonged here. When my mother
died, I couldn't make it to the funeral. I got there when all was
finished. Afterward, I couldn't express my grief with portraits
(I'd spent a substantial portion of my career painting portraits),
so I found another way. I did it through abstract. And I loved
abstract for that.

As a portrait painter, it is much harder to do exhibitions.

Rarely are people interested in someone else's portrait. So, as an abstract painter, I had the opportunity to have my first exhibition in New York in 2006. My father traveled from Iraq to Jordan and then flew to the US to attend. My daughters were already in the States, so it wasn't difficult for them to be there. But my son was across the world and came to surprise me. I don't even know where he had come from.

WN: How did Living Light International come to be?

QARAGHOLI: I've always wanted to give something back to life, always, but I didn't know where to start. My father was my hero, a big influence in my life. He gave us everything while he was alive, didn't wait until he was gone.

He had cancer and asked that I bury him in Iraq after he passed away. I couldn't bury him there because of the kidnapping and violence, so we buried him here. After his death, I went through a hard time. Then I had an idea. My paternal grandfather died when my father was six years old. Although my father still had his mother and his family, he told me of the misery he felt because he didn't have a father or anyone to completely depend on. This deep wound inside of him is why he gave us all the love that a father could give.

So I decided to start Living Light International for the orphans in Iraq, and once it started, God took over. He guided us. I go to places in Iraq that most people are afraid to go to. It's no man's land, but I go. My goal is to empower the street children, to build their self-esteem, to teach them tolerance and nationalism. I want to teach them how to be sympathetic to the poor and toward the world at large, not just the country of Iraq. A lot of the children we worked with who once wandered in the streets returned to school. They felt motivated and realized that they can improve their situation. I have taken doctors with me from America to do heart surgery in Iraq. We rescued 962 children whose lives were in danger.

They all call me Mamma Nadwa. Because of those kids, the art that I was completely involved in started growing and I found other venues to explore. Through trying to help those kids, the horizons increased.

WN: How much of your time do you spend in Iraq?

QARAGHOLI: Last year, I spent six and a half months in Iraq. Before that, eight and a half months. I spend a lot of time there because it's more important to be there. It's about there. It's not about me. During these visits, I have established a base, even though I don't have employees. I only have volunteers. We don't take any funds from anyone, not from organizations or governments. I take services. I pay for my travel and expenses and whoever comes with me pays their way as well. With all the corruption happening in Iraq, the reason I was able to succeed is because I work for free, so everyone trusts me and is willing to work with me.

I feel that God took something very dear to me, my father, but He gave me something very powerful which I have been after. Some people never know why they are on this earth. I know. I really, really know.

When I started painting, it was all about what was inside of me, my own feelings and visions. Over the years, I found myself combining the arts with community service. That's how we came to our most recent project, *Make a Wish.*

WN: What is Make a Wish about?

QARAGHOLI: A wish is the beginning of a goal. I'm trying to inspire kids, through art and painting, to set goals for their lives at an early age so they'll have a purpose rather than a day-to-day lifestyle. I'm trying to help them discover a vision for their future, one they can happily pursue. Our mission is not only to help the children in Iraq, but to expand to other regions. I don't feel confined to one place. I feel I am connected to the world. For several years, I worked locally with people in the halfway house, helping addicts find jobs. They called me Mrs. Q. I love doing humanitarian work, but as an Iraqi-born, I am able to reach out to the Iraqis because I understand them.

I started Living Light International because I felt the need to do something. This is my way, my solution. It's what I'm capable of doing. It's through art that you can feel the humanity of the other side. My passion is for the arts, plus for Iraq, plus for America. I want Iraq and America to understand each other. I really do.

WN: Why is it important for them to understand each other?

QARAGHOLI: The 2003 US-led war failed because the Americans did not know the language, the culture, or the history of Iraq. What good were all the sacrifices that America made during the war on Iraq? People need to ask themselves that question.

Many people have only started getting acquainted with Iraq because of war. For a long time, Americans had no idea where I was coming from. They didn't believe that there are independent women in Iraq. From the beginning, they knew who I was, but they couldn't match that picture of me with that part of the world, especially with Iraq. Maybe they think I'm exceptional or not the norm.

I want to create programs where children here learn about children there so they learn firsthand and not through the media. The world is ruled by a few media outlets and that's a scary thing for our children.

WN: Your paintings are full of life and energy. Do all your paintings have that, whether or not you are feeling sad?

QARAGHOLI: Yes, that's me. Even when I start feeling sad, I still see life with a colossal and happy picture. There's death, but there is childhood and hope.

WN: What is the story behind The Cycle of Life?

QARAGHOLI: *The Cycle of Life* is oil on canvas. I painted this about twelve or thirteen years ago. It was inspired by Omar Al Khayyam. When I could not make it to Iraq to attend my mother's funeral, I went through a sorrowful time. I acquired the somber mood that Al Khayyam is known to have and I could not get out of that mood. Al Khayyam had a rubai that talks about how, after a rooster crows, people who are at the entry of the tavern door beg entry. They say, "You know how little while we have to stay, and once departed, may return no more."

This means that once a day is over, it's not coming back. You have to live your day, make the most out of it. On the left-hand side of the painting is a fruitful, happy, and colorful tree. On the right-hand side, the same tree becomes old and dry, but the large hand, its roots, is still gripping to life. They don't want to let go.

The masks under the arch are people who come to this life wearing masks because they try to hide their real feelings and their real faces, having grown up with the words "No, no, no." In an oppressed society, you cannot show your opinions or true feelings.

Underneath the masks is a coffin of kings. Even kings, no matter how powerful, are going to die. What remains are their deeds, documented in a book.

On the side of the dying tree, there's one apple still hanging, still tempting. A human, until his death, is tempted by and holds onto the greed of the world. Trying to give back to society and, at the same time, desire the materialist world is a struggle from beginning to end.

Look at the wheel of the cart, the wheel of life. The wheel in the front is bright. That's the male. The one in the back, which is in the dark, is the female. I feel that this is one of the weaknesses of our Eastern society, that the woman is not given her true role in the world. The future is solely for the man. The women, half of society, are left in the dark, and yet it is that half that is raising the new generation. If women are left in the dark, how is the new generation expected to learn the light? If she's ignorant, she can't raise enlightened kids. How can she give them something she does not have? So the cycle goes on and on. Darkness brings darkness.

But still, me and the people I work with, we have hope. That's why we take care of the younger generation and enlighten them. This is the purpose of Living Light International. We want to replace darkness with light.

To learn more about Nadwa Qaragholi's creative endeavors through Living Light International, visit www.lliinfo.org

Top – Wheel of Life

Bottom – Shadow Show

Top – Beneath the
Summer Dresses
in New Bloom

Bottom – Samara-
Infinite Yearning

12

RANDA RAZOKY

Randa Razoky was born in Baghdad, Iraq. She had her first art exhibit at age nine. She received an Engineering degree from the University of Baghdad and had a job at the Ministry of Oil while developing her art. Her paintings reflect Mesopotamian culture and folklore and natural beautifiers such as flowers and landscapes. She left Iraq after the 2003 US-led invasion. She lives in Michigan with her ten-year-old son.

WN: You had your first art exhibit at nine years old?

RAZOKY: Yes. When I was nine years old, my family was invited to attend a famous art gallery by an Assyrian woman artist, Najat Jarjeas. I was so jealous of the art gallery that I told my father I wanted my own gallery. He said, "Okay, start painting." So I did as my father suggested and when I had enough paintings to exhibit, we invited family and friends to my first exhibit. It was a small exhibit, but it gave me confidence. The next morning, before going to work, my father wrote me a heartfelt letter and gifted it to me along with a book called *Learning the Principles of Drawing.*

WN: What did the letter say?

RAZOKY: I will tell it to you in Arabic and I'll have my father later translate it to you in English:

My dear Randa, blessed be your days.

This is my present to you after your insistence to enter the world of arts yesterday through the preparation of your simple and personal exhibition when you gathered all of our clan to see samples of your work. This is the first step, my dear, and it makes us all very happy: myself, your mother, and all your kin. You will find support from me personally in all the efforts to help you choose the path you want in your life.

I write these lines at ten o'clock in the morning on Saturday, January 12, 1985, while looking at a famous saying: "A person should immerse himself in the madness of work because it is the only pleasure that continuously grows until death."

We hold great hopes for you as well as for your sister, Suereth, to be great examples. With our hopes and wishes for your success.

Your dad,

Salem J. Razoky

Randa's first exhibit at age nine and her father's letter of support

WN: What influence did your father have in your life?

RAZOKY: He had a big influence. He was an intelligent and successful man who, in 1961, received a scholarship from Iraq to study at the Colorado School of Mines. He attained a degree in Geophysical Engineering from there and a Master's of Science from the University of Baghdad. After I graduated with an engineering degree, I worked with him at the Ministry of Oil, where he worked from 1967 to 2007, a total of forty years! He then retired, but he was later approached to manage a petroleum company in northern Iraq.

That simple gallery that he made possible for me gave me a big push forward and created a confidence that spilled into other parts of my life. At the Ministry of Oil, his friends would often say to me, "Oh, we remember you from that gallery."

WN: What happened after that first gallery?

RAZOKY: I continued to draw and in 1988, I won best caricature contest in elementary school. During my high school years in the 1990s, there were sanctions on Iraq and it wasn't as easy to attain certain art supplies, so I started painting T-shirts, jeans, accessories, and greeting cards.

After high school, I attended the University of Technology, majoring in mechanical engineering. I was chosen for that field based off the scores on my tests. My dream was to be an architect. Architecture is portrayed in my paintings. I'm really influenced by that.

WN: How did the war affect your art?

RAZOKY: I am a very sensitive person. What has been happening in Iraq really hurt me. I was twenty-six when I left Iraq. The Ministry of Oil was hit one day, the missile going right into my office, and the next day, my team and I left Iraq.

When you are forced to flee your country, much sadness remains inside of you. My paintings became very sad.

I once painted a painting of mosque, churches, and Mandaean men baptizing women by the river, where the Tigris and Euphrates Rivers flow. This painting represents an Iraq of diverse religions which no longer exists. We lost that Iraq.

WN: Did you continue to paint after you left Iraq?

RAZOKY: No, I did not paint between 2003 and 2006. After I left Iraq, I got married and had a son, who is ten years old now. My marriage did not last long. In 2005, I applied for asylum in the United States and in January 2006, I was accepted. When I received the notice, I was so happy that I cried for two hours. I began to enter exhibits and this rejuvenated my passion for art. The year 2006 was good for me.

WN: You've done quite a few art pieces which incorporate a dove and flowers. What does the dove and flower represent?

RAZOKY: These are watercolors which I started to paint in 2007, during Iraq's civil war. The one with the peach flower is called *Shlama*, peace. I was very sad and disappointed about what Iraq was going through. This flower gives a little hope. It says that in dark times, there's still hope. Your country is still beautiful in your eyes. The dove is the male, because to bring peace, you need a brave man. The flower is trimmed because even peace is not one hundred percent complete. It can't be.

The one with the white flower is called *Shayna*, security. The dove is a quiet female and she is surrounded by blood (the small red flowers). She is shy, scared, and is white and blue, like a baby. It's not a full flower. Part of it is cut off because even if you have safety and security, it's not one hundred percent. There's always a criminal somewhere. But ninety percent safety is great.

Peace and security should come together like man and woman. You can't separate them.

WN: What about the painting of the village?

RAZOKY: That's my grandparents' town of Alqosh. I went there twice a year during my childhood. Our family has two homes there. Alqosh is a big and ancient town that is known for its old arches and lots of steps. Its stones are mostly a gray and beige color. The level of its windows, even on the same house, is not the same. It's situated over Nineveh's northern plateau. If you stand at the bottom, you can see the slope and Alqosh at the top of the mountain.

The Alqosh in my painting, which is colorful, is not how Alqosh looks. This is how I see it.

WN: What about the painting of the old woman in the house?

RAZOKY: That's my grandmother wearing a traditional purple house dress. This is our old family home, which is a hundred years old and still standing in Alqosh. She is on the third floor, and the grapevines in that painting are coming up all the way from the first floor. My grandmother loved to plant grapevines wherever she went.

The child in the other painting is me. My grandmother lived with us and spent a lot of time with me because my mother worked as a librarian in Baghdad.

WN: Alqosh is a Christian town in northern Iraq. Many Christians fled there for protection after the Islamic State attacked their towns. Is it still safe in Alqosh?

RAZOKY: Yes, it is safe.

WN: Where do you plan to take your artwork?

RAZOKY: I want my time mixed between engineering and art. Engineering is very structured and art is more flexible and free flowing. I want engineering to complement art. I'm a very clear person, so when I paint, I want that person looking at my painting to understand what the painting is.

In July, my work was part of an art exhibit where I saw a painting by Qais Al Sindy. It was of a countryman and his wife. The woman was holding a bushel of palm dates. It was such a beautiful painting that it brought tears to my eyes. I thought, he must be so sensitive to have depicted such a touching painting. I could not stop thinking about that paining even after I returned home. I almost wish I had not seen it, it affected me so much.

Top – Alqosh

Bottom left – My Home

Bottom right – The Land
Between Two Rivers

Top – Shayna- Security
Bottom left – Childhood Memories
Bottom right – Shlama- Peace

13

ZUHAIR SHAAOUNI

Zuhair Shaaouni graduated in 1974 from the Baghdad Institute of Fine Arts with a degree in art. His medium at that time was painting. Photography was only a hobby. When he was a teaching assistant at the University of Baghdad in the Department of Art, he also worked part time for a newspaper, where he was required to take professional pictures. Some of his early photographs appear in his first book, *Memories from Telkaif,* published in 2006.

In 1977, Shaaouni came to the US to reunite with his

brother. He has since become a US citizen and a resident of Florida. He continued to work in art. The technology revolution of the 1990s opened up a new field for him. That is when he began to work in digital photography.

He exhibited his first digital work in 1999 at the Urban Park Gallery in Detroit. The new medium energized his creativity. He found great freedom in it, and for over two decades he has considered himself a digital artist. When he participated in the Bagley Housing Art Gallery in 2009, he exhibited his first works in color.

Shaaouni chronicles his experiences in his striking photographs of the aftermath of war, depravation of freedom, and daily accounts of the unpredictability of life, the beauty of nature, and the simplicity of recalling memories. He has committed himself to "rediscovering happiness." His mission is not just for himself, but for all people. He wants to lead humanity to a better state of mind and spirit.

Shaaouni's work has been exhibited in Baghdad, Prague, Paris, Detroit, San Diego, Washington DC, Cairo, and a number of other cities around the world. He has been invited on many occasions to act as juried artist adjudicating other artists.

WN: What was your childhood like in Iraq?

SHAAOUNI: We were raised in artistic freedom. Our house was full of bookshelves, CDs, music, radio, and politics. My father, Jirjeese Petrus Shaaouni, cared about his library of books as much as he cared about his seven children. So naturally, my siblings and I had an interest in the arts, but I had more of an interest than the rest.

My father had a law degree, but he worked as a mail warden in the town of Telkaif. He also read and wrote letters for people, since back then not many knew how to read and write. He spent his life between his work and the world of art and culture.

WN: When did you start drawing?

SHAAOUNI: I began drawing in elementary school. Once my math teacher slapped me, called me a fool, and told me I would die of starvation because of my preoccupation with drawing palm trees instead of focusing on math. Incidentally, he was also our art teacher and a good artist, but most art lessons ended up gone with the wind. Instead of teaching art, he used that time to have us do more math because, he'd say to the students, "You are behind with the curriculum and must catch up."

I went home and told my father what the teacher had said and done and my father told me to pay attention to my lessons. The next day, he brought me a box of watercolors and reiterated that I pay attention to the math teacher at school and to draw at home. I always remember this incident because it signifies the importance of an educated father to the genesis of his children.

WN: What type of artwork do you do?

SHAAOUNI: I graduated from Baghdad's Institute of Fine Arts, a prestigious school founded in 1936 from which many artists in the various branches of art graduated. Everyone knew me as a photographer because I had a passion for photography, so I, for a while, abandoned drawing and worked as a photojournalist in several Iraqi newspapers. I learned a lot from those jobs. I later taught at Baghdad University. There were a number of good students who really excelled in sophisticated and beautiful photography work. During that time, I participated in many exhibitions both inside and outside Iraq. In 1969, I won first place in an Iraqi exhibit for young photographers.

Since 1985, I have been experimenting with digital art, and in recent years, I accomplished a lot of successful projects in this area. My first exhibit in digital art was in Detroit at Urban Park Gallery, an old building that used to be a leather store in 1936.

WN: Who were your influences and what was your inspiration?

SHAAOUNI: I am not influenced by one particular artist, and my art belongs to me and does not belong to someone else. I do owe much to my high school art teacher, Behjat Abosh, and to my brother, Thamir, who does ceramics. With no doubt, I also credit my beginnings to the legendary artists who preceded me and my teachers, and let's not forget that a human is influenced by his surroundings. Recently, I have been inspired to make abstract art by the new art classes I was introduced to.

WN: When and why did you leave Iraq?

SHAAOUNI: I left Iraq in 1977. There's no reason why I left. I ask the question, "Do all those who leave their country have to have a reason to leave?" I was in good economic and social position in Iraq and I simply wanted to go out and see the world and learn from others in order to advance my abilities. Is there anything wrong with that?

WN: How has moving from Iraq to the United States influenced your artwork?

SHAAOUNI: Transitioning to a new life is never easy. The lifestyle here is different. The streets are different. Cities are full of cars and tall buildings. Men hold beautiful women by the arm, and hundreds of other new things which I had never seen before. I had to start brand new and learn where to buy what I need and search for stores. Little by little, things got better and easier and I began to fit in.

Later I went to California in search of a cultural life. I did an exhibit in Al Cajon and another one in San Diego, which featured works from some of the most influential Iraqi artists, such as Maher Al Samarrai. These exhibits brought me back to life.

WN: What has been your biggest challenge in your art career?

SHAAOUNI: That's a beautiful question. Selling my work! I can't describe the joy I receive when I see my work chosen and purchased at an art gallery by people I don't even know. That this artwork will reside with their family brings me true happiness which no amount of money can replace.

WN: What are you currently working on?

SHAAOUNI: I make my living from print and design. I give a lot of my time to digital art because it's the art of the future, or rather, it's a path that has found its way to peoples' lives and is progressing rapidly along with the other art forms.

WN: What do you hope to see in the future for your artwork?

SHAAOUNI: I can't foretell the future. Every day I work to improve and develop my digital artwork. An artist aims to make sure that his work is distributed. One thing I know is that I have a book coming out this year called *Ruwa*, which contains eighty-five of my digital works. My first book, as you know, was *Memoirs from Telkaif.*

When I was working on *Memories from Telkaif,* I wanted to preserve the town of Telkaif that is now destroyed. I wanted our children to know their roots. I delivered a letter to the current generation that they have roots in Iraq in a town that was built by their forefathers. *Memoirs from Telkaif* helps us see how our ancestors lived. Now Telkaif is a dream. In 120 pages, I was able to preserve Telkaif.

I also have a collection of photographs of Alqosh. I wanted to publish those as well, but I needed more pictures. When I was in Iraq, I considered going there to take the additional pictures, but I was too afraid to return to that town. It was dangerous. Maybe next year.

WN: You recently visited Iraq. What would you say is the biggest difference today from before?

SHAAOUNI: I went to Iraq from February to June of 2014. Life there is very different now. Before, there were schools for the arts. Now there are no schools for the arts. Now there is no such thing as freedom. There used to be structure. Now there is not. Even the students hit their teachers. Now no one around the world acknowledges a master's degree in Iraq like they once used to.

In the four months I was there, I did an exhibit. One of the art pieces was called *Sadness* and the minister of education asked me, "What sadness?"

I said, "Sir, Iraq is sadness."

Top – Baghdad Moon   Bottom left – Divine Pot   Bottom right – A Virtual World

Top – Mazes Cities
Middle – In the Prevalence of Salvation
Bottom – Window In A Forest

Pictures from Memoirs of Telkaif

Inside of the Church of
Sacred Heart of Jesus

What used to be the Flour Mill of
Al-Bitty. Now a residence.

Bright stone Cemetery

Girls congregating in front
of house entrance

14

RENI STEPHAN

Reni Stephan was born in Baghdad, Iraq, in 1981. In hopes of a brighter future, his family decided to leave their home country ten years later. Their dream became a reality when they entered the United States in 1993. Stephan was immediately enrolled in elementary school. With his new opportunities, he discovered a profound love for drawing. From an early age, his talent was undeniable. This continued throughout his childhood, and upon entering high school, art became his priority. Taking many classes in this field, Stephan's interest expanded. Slowly, he began to realize that he could merge his passion for art with the dedication he had for the culture he had left behind. He attended Detroit's College for Creative Studies in 2005, where he furthered his reach and began painting and sculpting. Inspired by Western art, as well as legendary artists, Stephan decided to dedicate his life to his crafts.

Stephan turned his family's garage into an extraordinary studio, where, during the winter, he used a furnace to keep warm as he worked, sometimes for a consecutive ten hours. In the summer, he opened the garage door and enjoyed the fresh air and natural light as well as the people who literally stopped their cars and came down to ask him questions. People in the neighborhood know who he is and what he does. He liked that—not for the attention, but because this gave him the opportunity to introduce the subject of his work, which mostly represents Mesopotamian history, to those who do not know about this history. As his work expanded, he was commissioned to do bigger and more complicated projects and this required him to rent out a studio.

With each piece he creates, Stephan's hope is that he will remain true to his Assyrian Babylonian heritage and ensure its survival. Not only does he seek to move generations of Assyrians, but he hopes his work will inspire all people of the world.

WN: How has your family reacted to your career choice?
STEPHAN: I come from a family of artists and vocalists. My father, Sami, is a well-known singer and professional guitarist, so I had tremendous support and a number of influences

growing up, first and foremost my paternal uncle. My father, who is Assyrian, is in constant awe of what I do. Every time he sees my completed artwork, he says, "Don't sell this one, Reni. Keep it for the house."

My mother, who is Chaldean, also loves what I do, but she's around it so much that she now sees it as normal. Both my parents taught us not to forget our history and culture, so I try to reflect that in my artwork. I feel it makes a difference. My dream is to one day inspire the world with my work and to help my culture in every way possible.

WN: How has the community received your art?

STEPHAN: Our people are well-educated, but they need to learn more about their own history. They've struggled for so long that they haven't had time to observe and appreciate art. They couldn't represent and place focus on their history because Saddam wouldn't allow it. I remember Iraq always being in a war, my father in the army, and my mother worrying about whether or not he or my brother would come home alive. Now that we are free, I try to show our people about us. Here in Michigan, I take my sketchbook and visit museums at least three times a month.

I recommend that everyone get more involved in the arts. The world is made up of art. Art is in cars, clothes, everything. Art is very educational and if people start learning about it, they will really get addicted to it.

WN: So, you see your art as a form of service?

STEPHAN: Yes, but I don't serve my community solely through art. I also serve it by getting involved in various organizations, like the Assyrian Aid Society, and by donating art pieces to the church. I'm following in my parents' footsteps.

They're active in charity work. Before, I couldn't wait to visit Iraq, to see relatives, and, of course, Iraq's famous ancient cities, its landmarks, and its national museum. Now it's a whole other matter.

WN: What kind of artwork do you do?

STEPHAN: I'm a painter and sculptor. I used to work with hydrostone and patina and even crafted wood-burning art. I had to stop doing this because the resulting smoke I'd inhaled for two years was affecting my health.

WN: Your work appears in numerous Iraqi establishments. Can you tell me a little about that?

STEPHAN: Many in our community have commissioned my art pieces. Inside Bellagio, there are two large statues, one depicting King Ashurbanipal of Assyria and the other depicting Gilgamesh, the fifth king of Uruk, holding a lion he captured. Inside Babylon Club in Warren is an eight-foot-wide statue of the *Babylon Lion* and a statue of the *Lion Hunt by Ashurbanipal.* I did a series of paintings of modern Assyrian and Chaldean singers, placing their images beside those of great historic Iraqi figures.

My biggest project is one I did recently. It took about five months to complete. It's inside Ishtar Restaurant, which is located on Fifteen Mile and Ryan Road. I had some help from a number of friends. For me, the challenge is not about making a living from my work. I'm able to afford the costs of materials associated with painting and sculpting. Regardless of whether or not I sell a piece, I am determined to continue my work. My challenge is about challenging myself. I like to learn and experiment.

When I was a kid, I dreamt of doing the large sculptural

pieces I did for Ishtar Restaurant. The *Mesopotamian Striding Lion* was my favorite piece. I had done one on a much smaller scale, but my dream was to do one that's even larger than the original. It's a very complicated, seven-feet-by-twenty-feet work. But once I accomplished it, I was very happy. That took weight off of me.

I've been commissioned to do artwork in Australia, Sweden, and other European countries. My next big project is creating three life-size bronze statues of Jesus and his two disciples, called *On the Road to Emmaus*. It's commissioned by the Manresa Jesuit Retreat in Bloomfield Hills.

No matter how good I perform, I want to improve myself.

WN: What do you do in your free time?

STEPHAN: Whenever I have some free time, I paint. I also help out with the family business that buys and renovates houses. And I have other hobbies. Even though I don't play a musical instrument, I arrange and mix music for my sister, Rena, who sings in our native language. We have a music studio in the basement where I work with Rena and her husband, a keyboardist, to produce her CDs. Not long ago, she went to Australia and made a CD.

WN: How do you feel about the Islamic State's attempt to destroy Iraq's historical monuments?

STEPHAN: Let them destroy it. We will rebuild it. After thousands of years, our history cannot be demolished, so even if they remove it from existence, its history will exist. Artists like myself will keep it alive and the new generation will be able to see it. Like myself, they will learn about Iraq's history from our artwork the way I learned about it from past artists. I'm very passionate about history and Iraq and I'm always excited to create pieces that portray that passion, oftentimes through modern methods.

WN: What is your vision for your work?

STEPHAN: I want to do enough commissioned work to raise enough money to have my own studio, a place where I can permanently stay and do artwork full time. In it, I would provide classes and workshops and have apprentices help me with my artwork.

15

SABAH SELOU WAZI

Sabah Selou Wazi was born in the town of Alqosh and moved to Baghdad with his family at age seven. He says that he knew from the time he could talk that he wanted to be an artist. At the age of seven, he used the razor of a pencil sharpener to make skinny figure stick carvings on chalk. While it was his dream to study at Baghdad's Institute of Fine Arts after high school, he knew he could not because, during that time, one had to be a Baathist or have two letters of recommendation from Baathists in order to enroll, so he went into the army instead and served from 1973 to 1974 in the civil war between the Iraqi government and the Kurdish government. Wazi left Iraq in 1977, first going to Perugia, Italy, then touring different parts of Europe until he came to the United States in 1979.

One of the founding members of the Chaldean Association of Fine Arts (CAFA), Wazi specializes in sculptures of Mesopotamia and paintings displaying the culture of the Babylonians, Assyrians, and Chaldeans. He has participated in many galleries and exhibitions throughout the United States and has won several awards. When 20,000 original artifacts were stolen from the Iraqi Museum in Baghdad, he decided to replicate the items, even though, he stated, it might take him three to five lifetimes to do so.

WN: How did art influence your childhood?

WAZI: I loved art and whenever I had small change in my pocket, like ten cents, I would buy chalk with it. I would use the razor blade from the pencil sharpener to carve stick figures on the chalk. The best gift I ever got was color pencils.

A lot of people tried to deter me from the arts. I would stay up late at night in my early teens, painting. My mom would say, "Go to sleep!" I would tell her, "No, I'm painting."

The next day, I would go to school and I would return home to see my paintings torn up. She wanted what's best for me, but what she thought was best for me was not what I thought was best for me. Today, I save whatever artwork my children create.

After high school, I couldn't go to art school because during that time, you either had to be a Baathist or you had to have a letter of recommendation or approval from the Baathist Party. The Fine Arts was very dedicated to the Baath Party. To them, if you were not Baathist, it meant that you are against them, so attending the school was out of my mind. I went to the army and served from 1973 to 1974 during the civil war between the Iraqi government and the Kurdish government. The Kurdish surrendered because Iran and Iraq came to an agreement that Iran would stop supporting the Kurds with weapons and such.

In war, you see your country falling apart and people from your country killing each other. In the end, nothing was accomplished from either side.

WN: You went to Perugia, Italy, after you were released from military service. What was that experience like?

WAZI: My friends lived in Perugia and I went there to study art with them. I lived with these friends for a month. That's when reality hit. I saw my friends were miserable there, with no jobs and hardly any money. My dream vanished in that one month. I couldn't maintain a living like that, so I started traveling around Europe, doing odd jobs. Then I went to Greece and applied through the Red Cross to come to the US.

WN: How did coming to America affect your art?

WAZI: Initially, I went to Dallas, Texas for a few months where I got a woodworking job. From the time I was twelve years old, I did furniture woodworking. In Dallas, I did the same type of work. I liked my job, was paid good at eight dollars an hour. But my friend who lived in Flint, Michigan, kept telling me I should come here, that he had a job waiting for me. I decided to leave Dallas and come to Detroit, where there's an Iraqi community.

I came to Michigan, and the next day, I told my friend, "Okay, take me to my job." He took me to a store in the inner city of Flint. I saw people coming in and out swearing, and I told him, "What am I supposed to do here? I don't even speak English."

The owner brought a milk crate, set it on the ground, and said, "Sit here and just watch if someone steals."

I was shocked and said, "This kind of job is shameful, to just sit and just watch someone steal."

I couldn't adjust and quit right away. I went looking for work, knocked on many doors, but I did not find a job, so I returned to that store. I worked there for a few months until someone in construction hired me.

WN: Did you have to abandon painting during this time?

WAZI: No. Even when I juggled two jobs, I always found time to paint. I would paint after work and oftentimes, throughout the night. The first painting I painted in the US was of a little girl playing the violin. I asked my boss, "Do you know anyone who would buy this?"

He asked, "How much are you selling it for?"

"Seventy-five dollars."

He gave me eighty-five dollars for it. This man became my friend and one day I was invited to his home with my family. It was a beautiful and extravagant home. I saw the painting I had sold him hanging on his wall. I offered to buy it from him for one thousand dollars, and he said, "No, I have a lot of good memories with it."

He had given it to his wife as a gift.

145

WN: What kind of art do you do and what influences you?

WAZI: I do figurative abstract sculpture and also oil paintings in large canvas. What influences me about art is...truly everything around me is art. When I was a young man I used to go to Baghdad Museum and I was very, very impressed with the art done by Assyrians, Babylonians, and the Sumerians. We know about our history from the art these dynasties left us with.

I took many semesters of art classes and studied two dimensional and three dimensional designs, sculptures, and oil paintings at Matt Community College, but I did not graduate. The major reason was that I had to make a living for my family. I visited many museums over the years and studied the art of the masters. I learned a great deal from their experiences, but the most influential artist and genius was Picasso. He opened all the doors for modern art and he liberated the art world.

WN: How do you see the Iraqi artist?

WAZI: We are not survivors. We are talented people who look forward to changing the world to a better place, a beautiful place to live in. It does not matter where you go, how far you travel, the artist's priority is art. I participated in many art shows throughout the years and every time I do an exhibit, it is a challenge that creates a new experience and inspires me to improve and grow as an artist.

WN: What are you working on these days?

WAZI: I do different sculpture and oil painting every day, some commissioned, some my own. I also enjoy doing woodworking. I would love to bring lots of historical pieces from our heritage to life with the help of sponsorship from our community.

WN: How did you feel about the looting of the ancient monuments of Iraq?

WAZI: I used to mostly create my own pieces, but the looting pushed me to rebuild what I saw before, replicas of Babylonian and Sumerian art, because a lot of people never got to see that.

One day a woman and her son came to my rug shop. After she left, she called me and said, "My son keeps bothering me to come and look at the artwork you have in your shop."

The boy was about thirteen years old, and when his mother brought him in, he said, "I'm interested in the Roman and Chinese empires." He pointed at one of my works. "Which one is this from?"

I asked him, "What's your name?"

"Yousif."

"Yousif, this is your ancestor's empire."

I taught him about Gilgamesh and other history that is not taught in schools, not even in Iraq, where in middle school, there was only one or two pages about Babylonians. The rest was about Islamic history. Yousif went home and Googled this information and was amazed by what he discovered. I made him an art piece. It's the Snake Dragon symbol of Marduk, the Patron God of Babylon, which is seen on a panel on the Ishtar Gate. His mother picked it up the other day. Doing historical art pieces has a great meaning for me because I'm educating people, but painting is my real passion. When I paint, I'm doing my own creation.

WN: What inspired you to paint Last Species?

WAZI: I was listening to the radio while driving and I heard birdwatchers talk about their experience in Hawaii.

They had watched a male and female bird for months. These birds were the last of their kind. Then, one day, the birds went missing. The birdwatchers looked for them and, several days later, found the male bird dead. They assumed that the female had also died.

Afterward, I kept thinking about these birds. I wondered what if the female bird had an egg, that egg hatched, and the baby bird knew he was the last of its kind on this earth? How would he feel to be without a mother or a father? Would he be scared? I made a painting of that chick and called it *Last Species*.

Top left – Beauty in Pain
Bottom left – Sound of Music

Top right – Goddess in Conflict
Bottom right – In the Wonderland

Top left – The Last Species

Top right – Fruit of the Day

Middle – Ancient Spirits Live

Bottom left – Seated Elegance

Bottom right – E…vil and the Apple

Top left – Liberty

Top right - Wooden 6-String Harp

Bottom left – Gilgamesh

Bottom right – Ashurbanipal Lion Hunt

16

SABAH YOUSIF

Many call Sabah Yousif "Picasso" because of his cubism-style paintings and extraordinary work. But Yousif's lifestyle does not resemble that of Picasso, whose revolutionary artistic accomplishments made him universally renowned and brought him immense fortune. For over twenty years, Yousif's lifestyle has been more like that of Vincent Van Gogh, who, unable to afford the use of models, purchased a mirror and went to work on a series of self-portraits.

Yousif was born in 1940 in Basra in southern Iraq. After having received only an eighth grade education, he was recognized locally as a child prodigy in the arts. He spent thirty-eight years in Kuwait, where his father had moved the family due to a job offer. In 1963 Yousif was given a position at the Free Workshop for Kuwaiti Artists, where he enjoyed a successful career until 1990. His pieces, which combine modern Iraqi styles and motifs with traditional images, have been displayed in numerous Arab and European capitals. He has been awarded several gold, silver, and bronze awards in the Kuwaiti Art Society's annual shows, and his paintings have been displayed in quite a few international, juried shows.

WN: How did your life change after 1990?

YOUSIF: I came to America for a visit and shortly afterward, the Gulf War started. I couldn't return to Kuwait nor could I return to Iraq. A relative advised me to marry a woman of US citizenship in order to stay in America. I took the advice, only to regret it for years to come. The woman ended up reporting me to the immigration office. Ever since then, I've struggled in this country.

WN: Did you ever consider leaving the United States to live elsewhere?

YOUSIF: A wealthy art dealer from France once offered to sponsor my work generously if I stayed in France, but I turned him down. I have no one in France. My cousins, whom I love dearly, all live here. But staying in the United States has brought me much heartache and hardship. Although I'm eligible to remain in the United States, having been granted "withholding of deportation" status in 2002, I do not have a Green Card and therefore cannot receive benefits such as disability and other government assistance.

WN: Your difficulties have not prevented you from continuing to produce incredible artwork.

YOUSIF: The subject of my paintings center around the human condition. I'm always incorporating, oftentimes with the usage of a dove, peace in the midst of wrestling empires. The faces portrayed on my canvases reject war and violence. I also incorporate a rainbow of colors that combine the region and culture of Iraq, Chaldeans, Assyrians, Syriacs, and Arabs (even using the Arabic script) to illustrate love, peace, and goodwill for everyone.

I once did a painting that depicted the horrific massacre that took place on October 31 inside the Lady of Salvation Church in Iraq. Other paintings have addressed the Amiriyah shelter bombing, where more than 408 civilians were killed during the Gulf War when an air raid shelter in Baghdad was destroyed by two laser-guided "smart bombs."

WN: How do you feel as an artist here in the United States?

YOUSIF: People here have, to my disappointment, little appreciation for my talent. They don't recognize the importance of art or of Iraq's great civilizations. I have won numerous awards from around the world, including one from UNICEF in 1989. I have had articles written about me in various languages. I sold countless paintings and freely and insistently passed out dozens to those who cross my path.

You see this award? *(He pointed to an award he received in the early 1990s).* If it was up to me, I'd throw this award in the garbage. It's not worth anything. I say this because I've been hurt, and badly so, to the point where I considered throwing myself out of my ninth-floor balcony. I've considered it on three to four different occasions.

When our interview ended, Sabah handed me a black and white sketch he had made. He said it was a token to remember him by. He then escorted me to the elevator and together we went down to the first floor. A number of Iraqi men and women sitting in the apartment building's lobby greeted him warmly.

WN: You have a lot of friends here.

SABAH: My friends and family love me dearly and I feel the same for them. I've survived and continue to produce work because of our genuine love and care for each other.

AFTERWORD

Artists have a story, a story that affects their pallets. The artists in this book support the bright side of an ancient land, Mesopotamia, a land which has been surrounded by negative perceptions for hundreds of years. These artists are not victims, but victors over their lives, following their passions and finding ways to showcase it despite any and all challenges.

The primitive forest is a frequent theme in Layla Al Attar's work and refers to the enchanted world of Gilgamesh, the ancient king of Uruk in Mesopotamian legend dating four thousand years, as well as the Garden of Eden, also believed to have been located in Mesopotamia. Iraqi-born author Buthaina Al Nasiri wrote that another favorite theme of Layla's was Adam and Eve, or the relation between man and woman and nature. Her paintings pictured wild trees entangled with the nude bodies of women.

Al Nasiri quoted an Iraqi critic and a friend of Layla, Suhail Sami, who said of her, "She did not like scenes of blood and violence. If you review all her work, you would not find more than one or two about war. One day, she showed me one of these paintings and waited for my response. The painting was about a massacre. It was filled with dead bodies but without a single shed of blood. The bodies were white and pale as if they had died of leukemia. Then Layla smiled and looked into my eyes, as if to say, 'No, you do not like such a painting, for you are like me, a peacemaker.'"

A journalist and newspaper editor who was one of her classmates at the Academy of Fine Arts, Anwar Al Ghassani, wrote this about her, "She was friendly, polite, warm, always had a smile, and above all, she was extremely beautiful. I don't clearly remember whether Layla was already married at that early age of eighteen or nineteen [when she was a student at the Academy]. If she was not married, why do I think that she perhaps was married? I don't know. Probably she was married and that was one reason why nobody in our group considered making serious attempts to attract her attention."

Layla Al Attar's achievements far outweigh the negative images that inaccurately described her. Zuhair Shaaouni said she invited him to her home to photograph her artwork. He described her as "elegant and kind." Amer Hanna Fatuhi said that she helped a lot of artists and families. He gave an example of her generosity.

"For six years, whenever we ran into each other, she would always greet me," he said. "I did not return the greeting. I liked her a lot as a person and as an artist, but I hated that she was part of the Baath circle. In the end, I discovered that she was a noble woman with a pure heart. When I tried to flee to Jordan, she helped me without letting me know she helped. Because she knew I'd refuse her help, she did it behind my back. That's how kind she was. I learned this from a friend who showed me documents that proved she played a role in my leaving Iraq."

Fatuhi said that her association with the Baath Party was not necessarily a political matter, but a smart survival tactic.

"Things are not always as they seem," he said. "In Iraq, many people became Baathists in order to survive and help their families do the same. They hurt no one. Becoming Baathist was their way of saying, 'Okay, we're with you, but we're not going to work with you.' Stupid people like myself confronted the regime and told them, 'You are bad.' That's why I got tortured.

"Had I known that, after all the sacrifices that I and others made, Iraq would be ruled by men like Al Maliki and Haider Al Abadi, I swear to God, I swear to God, I would go and kiss Saddam's hands. At least with him, we would have law and order. Yes, we lived in fear and he destroyed our lives by taking us from war to war, but at least you could go to church, hang out with your friends, drink and have fun without getting your head cut off. Had I known then what I know now, I would not have said a word. I would have gone to my studio and done my paintings."

Stories that distort the truth not only hurt people and countries, but they steal from readers and viewers the opportunity to witness true greatness, inspiration, and something very beautiful and relevant—reality. I hope *Iraqi Americans: The Lives of the Artists* opened a window to lives worth knowing and learning from.

Other books by Hermiz Publishing, Inc

IRAQI AMERICANS
THE WAR GENERATION

a collection of articles

WEAM NAMOU

the feminine art

{ a novel }

Weam Namou

IRAQI AMERICANS
WITNESSING A GENOCIDE

WEAM NAMOU

I Am a Mute Iraqi with a Voice
(ISBN-13: 978-0975295694)
A collection of poetry

Iraqi Americans: The War Generation
(ISBN-13: 978-0977679096)
A collection of 36 articles that Namou wrote over the years
which paint a picture of Iraqi Americans' political and social
situation and their struggles.

Iraqi Americans: Witnessing a Genocide
(ISBN-13: 978-0977679072)
A nonfiction book that provides the Iraqi American view on
Iraq and the Islamic State

The Feminine Art (ISBN-13: 978-0975295625)
A novel about a married woman who distracts herself from
boredom by trying to find her nephew a wife.

The Flavor of Cultures (ISBN-13: 978-0975295663)
A novel about a Chaldean girl in America who tries to find
her individuality while maintaining her tribal lifestyle.

The Mismatched Braid (ISBN-13: 978-0975295632)
A novel about an Iraqi refugee living in Athens who falls in
love with his American cousin.